THE INTEGRITY MOMENT

Making Powerful Choices in Life

Linda Tobey, Ph.D.

*Dorothy,
You are a
love! Be Big!
Linda*

KENDALL/HUNT PUBLISHING COMPANY
4050 Westmark Drive   Dubuque, Iowa 52002

CONTENTS

ACKNOWLEDGMENTS

The evolution of researching, writing, and rewriting this book over the years mirrors my own life transformation, both professionally and personally. This process, like the lifelong journey of integrity, features many people who have joined me, cheering me along the path.

My family and friends are the bedrock of my life—to my mother and father who have hoorayed at each milestone of my life, thank you. My grandfather, whose blessings are always with me, passed during this writing. No words express my feelings. To my friends Karen Gail Lewis, Kate Duggan and Linda Radoff, your continual passion, cheerleading and mentoring has meant so much more than words. My heart is full.

I also gratefully acknowledge my doctoral committee, who collectively served as rocks during the wild ride of discovery. Thank you, Barry Heermann, Don Klein, Dorothy Siminovitch, Susan Roche, Edna Kovacs and Sue Zabel. Thanks also to Mary Fambrough, who unselfishly and lovingly contributed to every part of the research process, and to Mary Finney for her energy and love in celebrating each tiny, flailing accomplishment.

No thanks is big enough for the men and women who participated in this study. As a story listener, I was rewarded with trusting accounts of the often deceptively simple, yet exceedingly rich, encounters with integrity in our everyday lives. Without that generosity, this book would not have been possible.

I am also grateful to the people who supported me in the creation of this book: editors Laurie Viera, Julia Taboh, Ilona Popper and Karen Speerstra. In addition, special thanks to Kathleen Erickson for publishing an excerpt in her excellent journal and

Kendall/Hunt Publishing Company. To Dianne Tesch, your energy and enthusiasm for me and this topic is beautifully projected on the cover of the book. Thank you.

Collectively, your spirits have made this journey of struggle and triumph not only enlightening, but also great fun. I hold the sweetness of this process in my heart. Thank you all.

INTRODUCTION

Just recently, I finished renovating a 1926 apartment in Washington, DC. Little did I know that the process of de-constructing and then reconstructing that space would transform my life.

From the first week in my new home, I began entertaining, teaching, sharing and working with groups of people in its commodious space. "It's so you, Linda!" exclaimed one friend. "What a comfortable space," commented a colleague.

Since living here, an abundance of love, friendship, business, wealth and happiness has been flowing freely. But perhaps most remarkable is the transformation of my often tense relationship with my father.

Less than two months after moving in, I hosted my parents for a rare visit, convincing them to stay with me rather than in a hotel. Then I set my intention for the visit to reflect the current Linda, just as my new home did. I visualized how I wanted us to be together, featuring me as patient and resourceful, kind and appreciative.

Over the course of that five day visit, my father recognized and acknowledged me for what felt like the first time. "You're really good at what you do," he remarked after watching me interact with my book group. "You're unique," he announced later that visit. As minor as those comments may seem, I was jubilant.

My sense of being Big during and after that visit is what characterizes an Integrity Moment. Whether a distinct event or stretching over a period of time, the Integrity Moment centers on our everyday situations, the choices we make and the outcome of our decisions. Successfully resolving life's dilemmas directly effects our sense of ourselves and how well we live a life filled with integrity.

The process of creating my home was about more than the resulting warm, welcoming living and working space. I evoked a wholistic, authentic expression of who I am and what's important to me. People recognize and respond to that expression.

More than ever, we yearn to bring our whole selves to the various roles and contexts of our lives. Yet, we often find ourselves living in the flurry of life—meeting deadlines others have set, fulfilling others' expectations, striving to achieve multiple goals all at once.

Living with integrity is not necessarily about ignoring these aspects of life. It's about acting with intention and choice. The more we make choices according to what is deeply satisfying, the greater our chances for living a "good life."

Better understanding the dynamics of integrity and learning how to create its resulting deep sense of fulfillment serves as the purpose of this book.

THE FRAMEWORK OF THE INTEGRITY MOMENT

The Integrity Moment represents choice points in our lives when something about who we are, what is important to us, and how we want our worlds to be are at stake. Each choice point may be resolved in a myriad of ways, including a sense of having integrity or a lack of it.

Typically, we want to resolve our Integrity Moments with choices that support and enhance our integrity. During this situation, the choice centers on *how* to act.

Experimenting in the moment, combined with reflection afterwards, helps us learn about our own style and challenges so that we can assess the choices that promote and inhibit having more integrity day-to-day. Over time, as we continue to learn from our experiences, we develop a Personal Tradition of Integrity—our unique collection of stories capturing personal themes and learning opportunities.

STORIES OF INTEGRITY

This book is full of personal stories—my own, stories of friends and family, and those of participants in two research studies I conducted. All these stories illustrate the different ways in which we can learn about and create a Personal Tradition of Integrity. Filled with both human failings and personal triumphs, these stories invite comparisons to your own life and offer inspiration and guidance on your quest for integrity.

Indeed, listening to many stories of Integrity Moments has provided me with the freshness of perspective, of looking anew, at my own experience. I'm reminded not to get stuck in my own way of thinking and my own way of seeing the world. As a story listener, I appreciate both the uniqueness as well as the similarities of each of our experiences.

Listening to stories of the everyday integrity of you and me is not only compelling, but is also important. They remind us to choose a little bit more mindfully, to live more consciously, to learn more intensely.

With an intention to hear diverse stories, I invited a broad range of people to talk with me. Inside of that diversity, I searched for themes that tie our differing experiences together. Those themes create the foundation for this book.

People from a variety of work and life settings participated. They included a construction worker, percussionist, teacher, therapist, hair stylist, college president, social worker, editor and a secretary. A machine shop manager, small business owner, consultant, accountant and social activist grandmother also shared their tales. All the stories are used with permission and feature alias names the tellers personally selected.

Their stories come from our everyday world and are not necessarily life-altering, Mt. Everest-climbing experiences. The almost unbearable sweetness of these everyday stories of integrity continues to touch me. Being inside the circle of an Integrity Moment is such a tender place, almost mystical.

The goodness of intentions that emerges in the stories, including those that demonstrate a momentary lack of integrity, is striking. Despite the evil, greed and violence in our world, after hearing these stories, I remain a complete optimist.

A WORD ABOUT KNOWING

You might think I must have all the answers and will provide you with a straightforward formula on how to fill your life with integrity. But like you, I'm in a continual process of discovery—a lifelong practice with the goal of leading a deeply satisfying life.

That said, I also recognize that in our Western culture, we operate with a basic assumption about integrity—that it is inherently a good thing. That cultural bias, founded in our Judeo-Christian, Golden Rule heritage, may be seemingly invisible, but is also pervasive. This assumption informs us all in our choice points.

The journey to a life of integrity is not simple or straightforward, just as integrity itself is not a static state—once achieved, always accomplished. Better understanding the dynamics of integrity, then acting on that understanding, is a continuing personal goal of mine and one I hope you find compelling both during and after reading this book.

AN INVITATION

The Integrity Moment: Making Powerful Choices in Life provides you with the opportunity to make your study of integrity personal. How does integrity show up in your life? What does living a fulfilled life mean for you? When do you experience yourself as Big?

In each chapter, two sets of tools support answering these questions. First, Strategy Time sections offer specific suggestions for mini-experiments and practical actions to extend your learning into daily life.

Personal Application tools present structures for reflectively applying the ideas presented to your own life issues. These exercises provide you with the opportunity to dive into the unknown and make it known, to jump into a confusion puddle and wash it clear, to express the previously unexpressed.

The exercises give you work space to explore your experiences. Journaling, meditation and other forms of self-care serve as additional ways to deepen your inquiry. The ideas in this book are intended to guide your own knowing. I invite you to weave in your tried-and-true methods of self-exploration to support your learning process.

Working with these ideas has changed my understanding of the world and has propelled my own learning journey into a wonderfully powerful place. I hope the same for you.

I also consider this book to be the beginning of a dialogue about integrity, the richness of its meaning, and its implications for living a good life. After engaging with these ideas, I would like to hear your response—what worked for you and what didn't. I look forward to learning more with you about our integrity.

Chances are you have some notion of what integrity means to you and that is what attracted you to this book. In Chapter 1, a definition of integrity and the groundwork for the Integrity Moment is laid out for you to try on, experiment with and continue your own exploration. The adventure lies ahead!

CHAPTER 1

THE DYNAMICS OF THE INTEGRITY MOMENT

Gary's close friendship with Stan and Susan, a married couple, has entangled Gary in a dilemma. Susan recently told him about her fears that Stan might be having an affair, but she hasn't confronted Stan with her suspicions. Within a week, Stan guiltily confesses to Gary in confidence that he is indeed involved with another woman.

Now caught in the middle, all of Gary's values and beliefs about committed relationships, friendships and loyalty come into conflict as he ponders his choices. Although he has known Stan the longest, Gary tends to sympathize with Susan. He can't help but compare Susan's pain to what he himself felt when he first found out about his ex-wife's affair.

Gary considers telling Susan what he learned from Stan, but that would violate a confidence. Maybe he would keep Stan's confession a secret, but also tell Stan that he wants to hear no more about it. Then Gary thinks he should also try to persuade Stan to be honest with Susan. But what if Stan continues the deception? Would Susan be angry with Gary if she eventually learns that he knew about the affair and said nothing to her?

Joyce, a middle manager in a large company, faces another sort of dilemma. Her boss, Ann, who can be both charismatic and autocratic, has just asked her to work overtime for the third time in two weeks.

She is concerned that what at first seemed like an unusual request for overtime is now becoming a habit. If she refuses to work the extra hours, she's afraid she'll upset her boss, and Joyce is easily intimidated by people like Ann.

On the other hand, Joyce has worked her way up from her beginnings as a part-time, entry-level assistant to get where she is in the company, and she would like to be further promoted. Being a "team player" by working overtime could help her career.

But Joyce's daughter is having trouble at school, and as a single mother, Joyce feels she should be there for her daughter as much as possible. She's already feeling guilty about working full time. She knows that whatever she decides will have consequences at work as well as at home.

These stories are just two examples of everyday situations which involve conflicting values and principles and decisions about how to act in the face of those conflicts. Integrity is about acting consistently with core values and principles. Yet, real life rarely presents completely straightforward choices for acting with integrity. As with Gary and Joyce, sometimes our deeply held, cherished beliefs compete, confuse and confound us.

These types of situations and choices represent *The Integrity Moment*—choice points in your life when who you are, what is important to you, and how you want the world to be, are at stake. Resolving a specific Integrity Moment, in turn, helps establish, refine and reinforce how you perceive yourself.

How to resolve the challenges of the moment differs from person to person. For example, how would you advise Gary and Joyce? Your choices in these and similar situations depend upon your values, how you interpret the circumstances, and what you anticipate would be the consequences of your action or inaction. As you can imagine, your choices may differ from mine, your colleague's, your mother's and your neighbor's.

The dilemmas may be resolved in a myriad of ways—leaving you either with a sense of having integrity or a lack of it. What you learn about the consequences of your choices instructs you as you move forward through life and encounter other similar situations.

This book focuses on how you resolve your Integrity Moments by helping you better understand both the dynamics of and factors affecting your ability to act. With that understanding, you can consciously choose to live your life filled with more integrity, day by day.

CHOOSING TO BE BIG IN YOUR LIFE

Typically, we want to resolve dilemmas with choices that support and enhance our integrity. These choices, even when made in the face of painful consequences, boost our sense of self-worth and self-esteem. They result in feeling Big about ourselves and our decisions. When we make choices that are inconsistent with our core values and principles, we are often left feeling Small.

Alice, in Lewis Carroll's Wonderland, has much to teach about size control. Curiously, she finds herself too big to go through a door and then, alarmingly, too small to reach the all-important key to unlock it. Miraculously, a potion with a labelled invitation to "DRINK ME" and a delicious piece of cake change her circumstances with her size.

Yet being big or small for Alice does not follow a consistent pattern. The drink doesn't always make her small, nor does the cake consistently increase her size. Peculiarly, even using a fan causes her to shrink rapidly.

Eventually, Alice finds a way to control her size, to make it just right for the situation she faces. A caterpillar advises her about eating from the right or left side of a particularly round mushroom to regulate her height. And clever Alice discovers which side is which. From that point on in her adventures, Alice can be whatever size she wants to be.

What does Alice's story have to do with moments of integrity? Quite wonderfully, a lot.

Each of us experiences two different stories: moments when we act *consistently* with our basic values and principles and those when we act *inconsistently*. In a Wonderland way, what separates the two experiences is a sense of how Big or Small you feel in the moment.

Quite simply, in the consistent experiences, 'I am Big.' In the inconsistent experiences, 'I am Small.' Happily, Alice helps teach that, with some effort, you and I can learn to manage our size, too.

Although you may not always recognize this quality in the moment, being Big or being Small is really a choice you make. Your choices provide a key difference between resolving your dilemmas into consistent experiences versus resolving them as inconsistent experiences.

Perhaps these choices seem straightforward or simple. After all, why not choose to have only consistent experiences? The fact is, real-life situations are very complex, often involving competing values and principles. We all have both consistent and inconsistent experiences almost every day. How you deal with these dilemmas shapes your Integrity Moments. Like Alice, you and I have moments of being both Big and Small.

Now, revisit the unresolved stories of Gary and Joyce. Remember how each is facing a tough dilemma, with no clear answers.

Gary has decided to talk with both Stan and Susan. "I thought my hair would turn gray overnight over all this. But I've decided to tell Stan that he needs to talk with Susan and to let him know that I'm going to say the same thing to her. Then I hope he'll feel the pressure to be straight with her." While Gary feels Big about his decision, "I plan to get the hell out of the middle of all this!"

Joyce is mired in indecision and overwhelm. Each day requires so much planning and organization that she is worn out from work and wakes up exhausted after tense evenings with her daughter. Regarding the overtime hours, Joyce, feeling Small, laments, "it takes so much energy to confront Ann, and well, I'm really scared to do that. I guess for now, I'll just ride it out. It will have to be OK."

GOING FROM SMALL TO BIG

In her Wonderland journeys, Alice had a few close calls. One time, she shrank so much that she wondered if she would disappear altogether, like a flame after a candle has been blown out. You may remember moments when you, too, felt that tiny.

Like Alice, you can make the choice to be Big again. As can Joyce. In another moment, at another time, she can choose to expand who she is rather than retreat into smallness.

My friend Mary, a committed vegetarian, told me about a pivotal family Thanksgiving gathering. She invited the whole family to her house, and being an inventive cook, I'm sure she was planning a delightful meal. Her family, knowing that Mary is vegetarian and keeps no meat in the house, said they would bring the turkey.

At first, Mary was torn about what to do. She certainly wanted her family's comfort as well as her own. She had always respected her parents' "superior role," such as abiding by a "no alcohol" rule in their house. Out of respect, she would never have considered bringing wine to a family dinner.

She decided to make this point with her family and share her vegetarian principles. She also joked, "the only turkey in my house will be sitting at the table and have a place setting!"

Mary's integrity in that moment centered on standing up for values that are central to her identity. For her, having meat in her home was as unacceptable as her parents having alcohol in theirs. She could have chosen to be Small and allow the family turkey to be served.

Instead, although awkward and a bit uncomfortable for everyone involved, Mary resolved her Integrity Moment in a way that left her feeling Big. And now, her family knows and respects her priorities as she does theirs.

STRATEGY TIME

When you find yourself in a Small situation, remember you can make another choice. The choice to be Big. Imagine what that choice would be. Even better, come up with two or three Big options.

Then, picture yourself as if you were living out one of those choices. Make a mental image of yourself enacting each option. Which is most appealing?

Now, step into that appealing picture. Imagine yourself seeing the situation through these new eyes, feeling how it is to make that choice. By experiencing this option, you gain the confidence to bring your Big choice into the real world.

THE NATURE OF INTEGRITY

I believe that each of us can have integrity—it is not the domain of a privileged, self-enlightened few. Neither is it a fixed commodity—once achieved, always present. We often find ourselves living with integrity in one moment, but struggling for it in the next. Therefore, integrity is inherently a work in progress: momentarily gained, a practice to develop for a lifetime.

Others may disagree. One prevailing psychological theory defines integrity as a phase of individual development, a point to be achieved. Specifically, integrity constitutes the final stage of adult development.

According to this theory, during this culminating stage of life, people reflect, integrate and make meaning of their life experiences. If unsuccessful, they tend to fall into despair. While integrity/despair issues may arise earlier in life, this process becomes predominant and is primarily achieved during later years, when other life issues have been successfully resolved.

I look at my aging parents and see this process at work. With varying degrees of success, they have redefined their lives following retirement, dealt with health uncertainties, and wrestled with age-related depression. I have watched the theory in action.

But I also know that even though I clearly am not at the final stage of adult development, I, too, have faced choice points when the integrity/despair dilemma was alive. When I am Big, I have integrity, while I fall into a kind of despair when I am Small.

6

Others think of integrity as integrating virtues such as love, wisdom, justice and courage. This definition implies that we must develop sufficiently to accomplish such integration and therefore it is only available to a few.

I would need all the years ahead of me to be able to integrate these cherished qualities. Our culture reveres heroes, such as Mother Theresa and Martin Luther King, whose images might reflect these virtues. But what about ordinary people? Can you and I overcome our fallibility to accomplish such integrity?

Intuitively, I know these elegant ideas do not fully capture my personal experience of and beliefs about integrity. I can look back over a lifetime of choice points that have involved values and principles. Certain moments like these capture our attention because they have something to do with who we are and what is important to us. I now think of these points as Integrity Moments.

Further, I believe both Big and Small moments involving our integrity occur everyday. They can even be overlapping, such as my relatively minor decision to refuse a copy of a pirated book and the larger-scale, extended set of choices about how to balance my life priorities.

Everyday integrity is not static or a quality some have and others do not. Just because we may lack integrity in one moment does not mean we cannot regain it in the next.

For example, I place a high value on and work hard to achieve individual well-being in my work and throughout my life. But if on the downtown streets where I live, I saw someone being threatened with violence, I am not sure how I would act. As a woman, I am aware of my own physical limitations.

Would I intervene? Go to a pay phone, and call 911? Yell for help? What is the relationship between feeling Big and personal safety? I hope that I would choose to help, in a safe way, such as calling the police or shouting.

For me to uphold my value as a creator and defender of individual well-being calls for my attention and intention. But my attention and intention are not ever-present. Even as I defend the well-being of a client, I may also blindly, inadvertently let another opportunity to live according to my values slip. In this way, our Big and Small experiences intermingle, and resolving life's dilemmas acknowledges and demonstrates our deepest humanity.

Similarly, no one has the corner on integrity. After all, you and I are human, with moments we are proud of and others we would just as soon forget. Yet, reflecting on those moments, we learn more about our own experience.

So rather than describing a developmental stage, integrity itself has a developmental quality—it grows and changes as you and I do. With each new experience, it is challenged, refreshed or momentarily reinforced. It is a life-long process of discovery and further creation, with recognizable moments in the journey. Integrity is not a specific destination.

STRATEGY TIME

When we have a moment that we label as lacking integrity, we may have a tendency to be hard on ourselves. Remember, that just because you may struggle with an integrity issue in this moment, life and your future actions will offer new opportunities to regain that sense of acting consistently with your values.

Practice accepting, and even loving, your own imperfections. Worry, guilt, and self-criticism are huge energy depleters. Try this reframe. Our mistakes and out-of-alignment moments are often the source of our greatest learning. From that richness we create an even deeper relationship to our own integrity.

GROWING WITH INTEGRITY

Integrity is a living, breathing phenomenon—developing throughout your life. Consequently, what might have been a burning integrity issue for you fifteen years ago may be quite different for you today. It may no longer even be important.

In my mid-twenties, I was most interested in establishing a career foundation and sense of accomplishment, which meant owning a home, excelling at my work, and achieving a certain level of financial security. During that period, I developed a powerful sense of who I was as a career person.

Then my priorities began to muddle. Dissatisfaction with the straight line of my career choices crept in. For several years, I danced around various new career directions, without ever settling on one. How about the Arts? The Social Services? Maybe the Peace Corps?

When asked what I did for a living, I sheepishly answered "marketing," quickly adding a disclaimer "but I'm looking for something I'd like better." I was feeling pretty Small.

At that point, balance in life meant learning to turn work off in order to develop other passions. I built a wall separating my work from the rest of my life and categorized the parts of my life—work as an energy drain, the rest of my life as inspiring. In time, through graduate school, my parents' illnesses, a cross-country move, and a serendipitous career opportunity that was totally new yet completely familiar, my priorities sorted out. I became clear about what was really important in my life.

While today a fulfilling, successful career is still important, I deeply value my relationships with my family and friends, freedom of expression, and a sense of personal awareness and development. Today, my integrity centers on acting according to these priorities.

If a conflict between one of these values and another part of my life occurs, then my integrity in that moment rests on supporting the central value. This choice may not be readily obvious, such as between good and bad options. It may rest on deciding between two good alternatives. For example, when I choose to turn down a freelance work opportunity because it conflicts with celebrating a family member's milestone birthday, I feel Big.

Integrity that develops with you allows you room to expand, change, and redefine your basic values and principles as you evolve. Over time, as you grow and become more self-aware before, during, and after your Integrity Moments, you may feel even more attached to some of your personal convictions, while others lessen in importance.

In each Integrity Moment, you have a choice—to act fully, in some degree, or not at all in a way that is consistent with your basic values and principles. In Chapter 2, you can explore more deeply the Big experience of acting with integrity.

FURTHER READING

Carroll, L. (1994). *Alice in Wonderland, Through the Looking-Glass and What Alice Found There*. New York: Quality Paperback Book Club. (Original work published 1865).

Carter, S. (1996). *(integrity)*. New York: BasicBooks.

Erikson, E.H. (1963). *Childhood and Society* (2nd ed.) New York: W. Norton & Company, Inc.

Kolb, D.A. (1984). *Experiential Learning: Experience as the Source of Learning and Development*. Englewood Cliffs, NJ: Prentice-Hall, Inc.

PERSONAL APPLICATION

Integrity involves acting consistently with what is important to you. Clearly, what you define as important shifts over time. Think about what mattered to you most five years ago.

What has changed since then?

What motivates you now?

What are the essential qualities in you and the world around you that make your life fulfilling today?

PERSONAL APPLICATION

Acting with integrity creates I am Big. Remember a time when you acted with integrity. Recapture that sense of being Big now.

Now, as if with a radio dial, turn up the volume of being Big, so that your Big becomes Bigger and Bigger, filling your experience completely.

Allow your body to memorize this experience.

CHAPTER 2

KEYS TO BEING "BIG"

In Wonderland, Alice learned how to be Big. By experimenting, she discovered that nibbling a particular chunk of a Wonderland mushroom would help her grow, and if she wanted, she could taste a different piece to shrink.

Delightfully, chunks of the mushroom are available for each of us, too. With awareness and intention, we can learn how to choose being Big during and after our Integrity Moments. Whether consciously aware or not, you choose how to perceive yourself in any situation. If you experience yourself as Big, you manifest the personal power to make it so. Similarly, you can choose to be Small, to abdicate some part of yourself to your situation.

We make choices during the Integrity Moment: whether to act or not and whether to apply conscious effort or act from habit. When we choose to take action and devote effort to the dilemma, we tend to demonstrate generosity of spirit toward ourselves and others. In contrast, being passive or reactive often leads to self-criticism.

In this chapter and the next, we focus on how your choices shift in the Big and Small moments. So come now. Enter the sphere of your everyday Integrity Moments, explore their simple complexity, and learn how to nibble your mushroom.

I AM BIG IN ACTION

When you nibble the Big chunk of the mushroom, you are likely to be active in your life, while the Small piece of mushroom leaves you feeling disempowered. In Big experiences, you act consistently with your basic values and principles and author the outcome of your circumstances. You are an actor, not an observer, taking responsibility for creating your own experience.

In other words, your personal power helps you produce your desired outcome. Empowerment is about passionately focusing on how you want to live and actively making the choices that bring that good life about.

Being in action has several qualities: taking a stand for change or in the face of opposition; speaking out to effect the situation; expressing a desire to influence someone or some situation; and establishing clear, firm boundaries for what is acceptable. You will see that the following stories often blend several of these qualities.

TAKING A STAND

Taking a stand to change or improve a situation, not accepting the status quo, is one key for being Big. Some definitions of integrity even require taking a stand in the face of opposition in order to have it. In this book, integrity is defined as acting consistently with your basic values and principles, so standing up and acting despite barriers demonstrates Bigness in the moment.

By taking a stand, you can be a catalyst for changing your world. Ron, a middle school teacher, was preparing to co-lead a zoo field trip for students. The other teacher took charge. "When we got into the room, I heard her instruct the class, 'once we get into the zoo, you are on your own. If a guard comes over to you, and asks where your teacher is, I want you to point over there and lie and say, my teacher is over there. Right over there.'"

"She used the word 'lie.' All of a sudden it hit me like a shock. I was in a very bad situation. I started to panic. I immediately went to the head of the department and told her that the teacher had instructed the kids to lie."

Although ultimately decisive, Ron did face a personal dilemma of choosing between two competing principles he holds dear: "I was thinking of the ramifications of reporting her, but one of my basic beliefs is that I should not 'turn in' someone who is my contemporary. But she behaved so badly that I told on her anyway, because another principle, my sense of caretaking for the students, superseded that." As a result of his choice, the other teacher was reprimanded.

His action created a temporary hierarchy of his principles, applicable for that moment, which allowed him to be Big. In another moment, he might choose differently. He seemed surprised, and pleased, that the other teacher "did not hate me forever, which I thought might happen."

SPEAKING OUT

Expressing what is important to you in a critical moment is like giving voice to your integrity. I remember the first time I used that voice, in my first Integrity Moment. I was twelve. Like any other pre-teen, I was shaped by the social forces of my peer group—their norms, preconceptions, and prejudices—and my relationships with them. How I wanted their acceptance, to be popular.

I only had one problem. I wore glasses. And at the time, glasses were anything but hip or fashionable. As Anne Lamott says:

> This is a difficult country to look too different in—the
> United States of Advertising, as Paul Krassner puts it—
> and if you are too skinny or too tall or dark or weird or
> short or frizzy or homely or poor or nearsighted, you get
> crucified.

No matter how smart or funny I was, and I was smart and funny, I did not stand a chance. I thought of myself as "hair and glare" from the mouth-full of braces, abundance of thick, wavy hair, and big, round, thick glasses.

During the summer between elementary and junior high schools, that summer when I was twelve, I changed. I got my braces off and finally, got to wear contact lenses. A pretty girl emerged!

The first day of school at junior high, one of the popular girls from my elementary school approached me and exclaimed in wonder, "Linda, you look wonderful!"

Without even thinking and with just a bit of a turned-up nose, I found my voice for the very first time and huffily replied, "well (dramatic pause), if you had called me over the summer you would have known," then turned and walked away, triumphant.

Junior high was good for me. I learned how to make friends. I experimented with very blue eye shadow. I spent an inordinate amount of time at the mall without spending a penny. I sang rock-n-roll songs, really off-key, with my girlfriends. I was learning who I was—my own person, not a follower.

Those moments of speaking my truth, staying close to who I am, come more easily to me now. Now, thankfully, I am much better equipped to speak my truth without offending. Yet, I may not remember any moment of standing up for myself as completely, body and soul, as that first time, that first day of junior high.

EXPRESSING A DESIRE TO INFLUENCE

Another quality of being action-oriented is the desire to effect the world around you. Mark, an activist who regularly writes letters speaking out against injustice, acknowledges his desire to influence the lives and thinking of others.

"On an ongoing basis, I write a lot of letters to congressmen, to newspapers, and for Amnesty International on human rights issues. I write to the head of the government, stating what I have heard about the case, my feelings about it and why I feel that it is an abridgement of human rights. I ask them to take some action, whether it is releasing the person, or investigating a murder."

Influencing on a personal level is satisfying, too. Susan wants to mend a family division that dates back many years. In planning a family event, she calls to invite her sister, who "just kept on telling me that she wasn't going to go, she wasn't going to go. I said, 'you don't have to make any decisions right now. You have got several months to decide.'

"Then I shared with her my feelings as to why I thought she should go. She knew where I was coming from, because I had just lost my father-in-law before the holidays. I just told her that it would be terrible if something happened and she hadn't talked to my parents for that many years." Rather than accept division in her family, she continued persuading her sister to soften her stance and reconcile with the family and ultimately was successful.

ESTABLISHING CLEAR AND FIRM BOUNDARIES

Taking a stand, speaking out, and influencing others all can help you establish clear, fair, and firm boundaries about what you find acceptable and what you intend to act on. Ron, the teacher who took a stand resulting in the reprimand of his colleague, set boundaries with the other teacher. "She certainly realizes that I will not go along with her cockamamie ideas."

Rick, a shop floor supervisor, takes a break from his computer to look out over the bright factory floor, watching goggled machine operators working and dusty residue flying. He is responsible for quality control of the company's products and continually finds his boundaries challenged, often pressured by the sales staff.

Today, "I stood firm on my ground and said, 'I am not letting that product go out the door. If I have to talk to the boss to make sure that this happens, I will because I can't send a product like that out with a good conscience.'"

Family situations can present difficulties in setting boundaries that allow you to be Big. As Brenda was planning her wedding to a man from a different religious background, she anticipated that her family wouldn't attend a church outside of their faith. She was especially concerned about her mother.

"But I wanted my wedding my way. So I was trying to think how I could make my mother happy and not fight with her on the most important day of my life? How can I show that I really believe what I have chosen? I said to her, 'I really think it would be best if we have it outside, in the garden at my house. I still would love you to help.'

"I stood by what I wanted. I really took a broad look at everything, at all of the possibilities here, because we had to try to please everybody. And please me." With her resourcefulness and firm boundaries, she created a beautiful, outdoor wedding experience that all her family felt comfortable attending.

STRATEGY TIME

When you notice yourself being passive during an important situation, take a moment to reconnect with what is important to you. Take the time to be clear about the outcome you desire. What compromises are you willing to make? What limits do you want to set? If you could tell one person your point of view, who would that be? Now, go do it. Every action pulls you out of passivity, invites you to take a stand, use your voice, and share your perspective.

What burdens are you carrying for others? Your mother's grief about not having the confidence to stand up for herself? Your father's worries that you don't make enough money? Learn from their concerns, then give them back. Keep your boundaries strong.

> **I am "Big" in Action**
> - Taking a Stand
> - Speaking Out
> - Expressing a Desire to Influence
> - Establishing Clear and Firm Boundaries

I AM BIG WITH EFFORT

Taking action is one way to be Big. Another involves applying conscious effort to resolve the dilemma. When facing a choice point, think through what is important to you in resolving the issue. That effort may involve considering how to act consistently with other similar situations and how to act consistently with your basic values and principles.

Your effortful behavior involves a level of deliberation and a sense of control over your actions that overrides any habitual, reactive, or automatic response that arises first. The results of your effort lead to setting intentions to be Big.

Phil demonstrates how applying effort helped him successfully resolve his work dilemma. Despite a customer complaint about damaged parts, several employees were certain the parts were actually mishandled by the customer. Normally warm and affable, Phil, as manager, faced a dilemma of whether to ship the customer new parts at no charge.

Looking noticeably stressed, he recalls, "my first reaction was 'no, I am not going to do it. This is not our fault. I know the parts weren't bent. I know they weren't scratched. No way. The customer threw them in a pile and trashed them. That is what they did.' I was so upset that this was even happening.

"Until I got my head together, had a cup of coffee and settled down. I had to get it straight in my head, which took all day. It just came down to no matter what the others say, we made the statement that customers are always right. So I came back the next morning and said, 'they are right, no matter if they are really wrong, they are right. Ship the parts.'"

Judith, a massage therapist, volunteers at an AIDS hospice. When a client asked her for additional massage time, "I guess my first inclination was to say 'no, I'm sorry, and I have to go. I have already spent over an hour, and I have got to get out of here.' But after thinking about it some more, I realized that he really needed the attention. That is important in this case, and I could stay and spend another ten minutes with him."

Aware of her instant negative response, she described a "conflict between my feeling concerned for him and his needs and needing to protect my own boundaries." She then elaborated on her internal process. "I kind of waffled back and forth for a little while. Not on a conscious level, but what I probably do is weigh my needs versus his and whether I am going to resent doing this later on, which is really counterproductive for both of us.

"I also try to judge how intense his needs really are, because there was obviously more going on than just what was on the surface." Reflecting on the situation and alternative courses of action, her process included checking in with her intuition and her values. Suppressing her initial response, she mindfully decided to give the client extra time.

EFFORT UNDER PRESSURE

Lydia, an instructor for a multi-ethnic junior college describes how she overrode her first response with a more effective, intentional way of handling a potentially explosive situation. One of her African American students made a racist remark in the context of a class assignment.

"Often, I can't get over my knee-jerk, almost elitist reaction, so that the first thing I want to say is 'that's not appropriate. I can't believe you said that.' There is this part of me that wants to get up on a soap-box and just ream somebody out like you would a little child."

Lydia noticed the palpable energy of the moment, which held the entire class' attention. "I realized everything was still. That there was no movement. No rustling of papers. Nobody was moving. It seemed like everybody literally was holding their breath. There was complete silence. It has never been that silent in that classroom before or since."

Lydia transcended her immediate inclination, paid attention to the kinesthetics of the class, and applied an effortful response to the situation. She questioned the premise of his statement, extracted content for support and separated the content from the controversial comment.

"He gave good examples. So, I said, 'you have got some good stuff there.' I wanted to have something solid before I caught him on the racist comment. I felt good about making sure that I pulled stuff out of him and did not jump on him right away.

"So as anxious as I was about his term, and I have a couple of Arab-Americans in the class, I wanted to first deal with the content. Then I shifted my tone, like I was giving him an admonishment. Maybe that was a little bit overdone, but I wanted him to realize that I was quite serious.

"I said, 'let's back up. It is not appropriate to be using any kind of racist slur. If it is important for you to say what kind of ethnic background somebody comes from, then somebody is an Arab-American or somebody of Arabian descent, not an A-rab.'

"Then I said, 'but having said that, the rest of your thesis is strong, I don't think you need that information. What you are picking on is a behavior. Not a person. People can change their behaviors, but they can't change where they come from. So, it is much more constructive for you to focus on behavior.' The rest of the class breathed a sigh of relief."

Lydia was handed what she describes as a "teachable moment" to role model her values and principles in a constructive, trust-building manner. With mindful effort and great intention, she resolved this delicate moment successfully.

STRATEGY TIME

Being effortful takes just that—effort. Practice being effortful. Take one hour out of each day and pay full attention to each of your choices during that hour. This kind of attention takes a lot more energy than we normally expend. That's why setting a limit on the amount of time you practice is helpful.

Notice just how many decisions you make during the hour. Keep a log. Pay attention to the scope and scale of the decisions. Which ones effect another? What choices do you have with each decision? Take the time to weigh the choices before acting.

Try this exercise for one week. At the end of the week, review your log. What have you learned about how you make decisions? What happens when you apply effort to those decisions? Building strength around your ability to apply effort when not under pressure will support you when you are.

I AM BIG WITH GENEROSITY OF SPIRIT

Being Big in our lives involves being active and effortful. Taking a stand for yourself and applying intention to the choices and decisions you make go a long way toward shaping your perceptions of yourself as Big in relationship to your world. Another feature of Bigness is also the result of this positive self-perception—your tendency toward generosity of spirit.

Bigness creates the space for generosity toward ourselves and others. Many of the stories here have demonstrated a generous spirit in several different ways. Willingly investing time with a person or activity is one form of generosity.

Carol willingly spends several hours each week helping her elderly mother with routine activities. Her mother "does not see very well which is why I go there religiously every day. Because I need to read her mail to her, and write her checks.

"I recently told her that although I do this partially out of a feeling of responsibility, I also do it because she's fun to be with. I enjoy her. She needs me to read to her. It must be sad when you get old and you can't see to do that." Carol demonstrates empathy—that feeling *with* another and receiving another into ourselves.

Empathy can help resolve Integrity Moments. What's going on for the other people involved in this situation? Being Big means having the openness to answer that question.

Clarice feels for both her son and daughter-in-law as they divorce. "It was very upsetting to me. But I managed to listen to both sides. I have a good relationship with my now ex-daughter-in-law. Of course, my son is my son.

"But, I think I'm a pretty objective person. And I listen to both sides without taking sides or with each of them thinking I was taking their side. I tried to let them know how I felt, that I loved them both, and that I was very unhappy about what happened, but I could understand what was going on."

TEACHING AND MENTORING OTHERS

Generosity is often expressed as teaching, instructing, mentoring or helping others, too. Hal, a project manager working with carpenters, gives them some advice. "'In order to rise above the rest of the competition, you have to have something special, something better than everybody else.' Naturally, they didn't know what the heck I was talking about. We were all gathered in a room, and they asked me to explain it.

"I said, 'for instance, when you come to work in the morning, and there is a customer there, or your peer is there, it's always nice to say good morning. How are you this morning? It's nice to have a shiny tool box, and all of the tools put away, not in a bushel basket, like I see some of yours—rust on them. It's nice to have clean clothing on, every day. To be clean shaven. And take care of your personal hygiene. Be to others as you would wish they would be to you.'

"So, probably 80% of them chuckled, said 'yeah, right,' didn't even give it a second thought. The other 20% said, 'hmm. What is the worst that can happen? Let's try it.' Well, the ones that did try it are still in business for themselves today. Little by little, they have been increasing their business volume and taking some of the customers away from the guys that have been in the business forever.

"They've come back to me, and one individual in particular has said, 'I will never forget that day when we gathered in that conference room, and you gave that spiel. Because every time I do what you suggested, I win. When I go back to the old ways, I lose.' So, that is the end of that story."

GENEROSITY REINFORCES BIGNESS

Stories filled with generosity of spirit clearly unveil core values and principles. In these stories, being Big creates a place for generosity, and a generous spirit creates a sense of Bigness for all involved. This circular relationship feeds itself, reinforcing and deepening over time.

I learned about how generosity cycles deeper and deeper during my graduate school experience at The Union Institute, which was rich, creative, fun and challenging. This educational period dramatically contrasted with my other advanced education programs.

I was continually delighted with the collegiality of learners who lived around the country, and the generosity we demonstrated toward each other, supported by a structure that sets up our serving on each others' doctoral committees. The system promotes cooperation rather than competition. I felt generous with my time, ideas, resourcefulness, creativity and depth of caring.

That generosity was tested at one point. One of my own doctoral committee members was over-committed in her life and consequently was unable to participate as she wanted on my committee. Rather than letting me know her situation, she backed off from communicating with me.

I decided I wanted her to resign from my committee, which represented taking a stand in creating my own learning experience, rather than allowing me to become a 'victim' of her overwhelm. The challenge became *how* to talk with her. With the support of other committee members, I developed a strategy. A strategy based on generosity.

When I spoke with her, I acknowledged how busy her life was and that our timing for working together was clearly off. As much as I knew she wanted to contribute to my work, I cared about her too much to create more pressure in her life. To preserve our overall relationship, I wanted to sever this part of it.

She was so grateful and relieved. Plus she indicated how much she had learned from our exchange, since she tends to withdraw and avoid confrontation.

That conversation allowed me to be Big, without making her Small. I feel triumphant that we both emerged from this generosity-based interaction in a way that preserved both our relationship and our dignity. The world is close-knit, and I know she is part of my future. If she learned from the experience, then perhaps next time, she will make different choices. Certainly I am learning how to, as well.

Generosity of spirit promotes successful resolutions of your Integrity Moments. By making space for the humanness of yourself and others, you can be Big. This generosity differs from the obligatory 'shoulds' in our lives, as I hope these stories demonstrate.

STRATEGY TIME

Being Big is about spaciousness. The openness of space allows for mistakes, frailties, humanness. Start by building spaciousness for yourself. And notice how creative your mind is.

If a circumstance leads your mind into imagining the crumbling of your future (I'm going to fail! I'm going to die!), notice first how small that space you inhabit seems. Your mind has just created some fiction based on anticipated, dreaded outcomes.

Expand the space by engaging the creativity of your mind further. If you have just created the worst case scenario, what's the best thing that can happen? Write some best-selling fiction, big and expanded and wonderful. Win an Academy Award!

Now that you have the best and worst case, both of which you may find humorous, you can find the middle ground. What is the likely case? What will really happen? Notice how much larger your sense of possibility is now.

With spaciousness for yourself, you can apply generosity to others. Think of someone you feel critical toward or have a problem with. Look down and think about this person. Notice how the feeling gets more intense as you focus downward.

Now lean back slightly and look up. Keep thinking about the person. What do you notice now? Maybe this problem isn't so bad after all.

Keys to Being "Big"

Integrity involves a Self-Perception Process

I am Big (and act consistently with my core values) when:

I am Active
- Taking a Stand
- Speaking Out
- Expressing a Desire to Influence
- Establishing Clear, Firm Boundaries

I apply Effort

I have Generosity of Spirit
- Volunteering Time
- Demonstrating Empathy
- Teaching and Mentoring Others
- Reinforcing being Big

This chapter has explored the characteristics of being Big in the Integrity Moment. Turn to Chapter 3 to learn what happens when you nibble from the other chunk of the mushroom. First, compare your own experiences with the qualities described here in the Personal Application tools that follow.

FURTHER READING

Branden, N. (1983). *Honoring the Self: Personal Integrity and the Heroic Potentials of Human Nature*. Los Angeles: Jeremy P. Tarcher, Inc.

Lamott, A. (1994). *Bird by Bird: Some Instructions on Writing and Life*. New York: Pantheon Books.

PERSONAL APPLICATION

Recall a recent experience in which you acted consistently with your core values and principles. Describe it here.

Who was involved?

What were you thinking and feeling?

What did you say and do?

What happened? What was the outcome?

How do the I am Big themes fit here?

What other factors were present?

PERSONAL APPLICATION

Recall a recent experience when you acted with generosity of spirit. Note it here.

Who were you in that moment? What qualities of you were present?

Close your eyes and take 2 nice, deep breaths. Let a song, image, or movement that represents who you are as a generous spirit bubble up from your unconscious. Record it here. Once a day reconnect with this touchstone of your generous spirit. Sing it loud, make the movements big, turn the brightness up on the image!

CHAPTER 3

WHAT KEEPS US "SMALL"

Now we nibble from the other side of Alice in Wonderland's mushroom, creating a very different sense of ourselves in the world. In this chapter, we look at what happens during experiences when we act inconsistently with our basic values and principles.

Unlike the Big stories in Chapter 2, these Integrity Moments result in feeling Small. Further, these moments of losing your sense of personal power and acting rashly or out of habit can lead to harsh self-criticism.

But don't fret. Even though feeling Small is not an uncommon experience, we will also explore strategies on how to grow from Small to Big.

I AM SMALL WHEN DISEMPOWERED

Just as being active and empowered is part of a Big experience, we may feel disempowered in our inconsistent moments. When we act inconsistently with our core values and principles, we can interpret our situation as being very Big and ourselves as quite Small.

Giving away our power gets expressed in several different ways. In some situations, we feel overwhelmed or stuck or unable to effect the outcome. In others, we withhold our own voice or avoid conflict.

FEELING OVERWHELMED

Stressed? Not enough time? Just too much to do? Got to balance everyone else's priorities with your own? How easy it is to attribute our behavior to these circumstances of overload. Blaming inconsistent experiences on overwhelm is one strategy for trying to get others to think favorably of you, despite your actions. And certainly overwhelm is a common experience many of us share.

At times, this strategy can come across as an excuse. "Because I am so busy and get myself involved in so many things, I make mistakes or do things wrong." "No matter whether I have an extra twenty minutes or I am five minutes behind, I always feel frantic, because I never feel prepared enough, because I am so stretched." Do these statements seem familiar?

Exhausted after a long day of work, Sue takes her son to the library. "My son took out a book that I didn't approve of. But I allowed him to do it anyway. I got the typical answer from him. 'Oh mom, it's just a book.' I decided to trust what I had taught him and allowed him to have his space. That night, I was just too tired to do otherwise."

Making choices takes effort. Taking a stand involves energy. In overwhelm, even these small situations become just too much.

Andrea, an attorney for indigent clients, suggests that case overload causes behavior that is inconsistent with her values. One client in particular irritates her because the client doesn't follow the actions Andrea recommends.

"My blood starts boiling. I just can't stand it because she is just one in a long line of people like this. If she were the only person like this, I would be very sympathetic. But when she is one of fifty, I get this sense that this is never going to end. I'm never going to get out from under this." These powerful feelings plague Andrea because she has consciously chosen her "good work."

STRATEGY TIME

Les Wyman at the Gestalt Institute of Cleveland refers to a continuum of overwhelm to underwhelm. Somewhere in the middle must be 'whelm.' So one strategy for dealing with overwhelm is to ask yourself, if this moment is over-whelm, then what is whelm? Take a moment and define what would be reasonable in this situation. What needs to shift for you to have whelm? What does whelm look, sound and feel like?

Recognize that sometimes your situation is like a tornado. Whirling all around you are people and objects from your life, plus maybe some stuff from who knows where? Where did that paint can come from? And that cow? Know that at the eye of the tornado is complete calm and quiet. Put yourself there now. Notice what affect that calm-quiet has on your sense of whelm.

Experiencing overwhelm can be dizzying, paradoxically leaving us immobilized. Finding whelm helps loosen that stuckness, clarifies priorities and creates a new sense of choicefulness.

FEELING STUCK AND LACKING CHOICES

"But I was stuck! I had no choice!" Perceiving your lack of choices gives great power to the situation and can certainly leave you Small. Viktor Frankl's personal recounting of his Holocaust experience served as my teacher about avoiding stuckness. I cannot imagine a more horrible circumstance, a more choiceless environment, than being imprisoned in a concentration camp.

He suggests that his survival was based solely on remembering choice. He teaches that we can always choose our attitude, even if all our other choices are literally taken away.

Yet in inconsistent experiences, you often can't imagine influencing the situation or finding other choices that would be more suitable. A critical stuck experience for me came during an Integrity Moment in college, over twenty years ago. Late one night, seated on our dorm's thread-bare, sprung-out couch, my boyfriend criticized my flirtatious behavior. "You know, you're not that pretty."

Stung, I sat in silence and listened to him rant. This young man was my first intimate passion. He was as important in my life as breathing. I had no idea he felt this way about me or my Texas friendliness, which apparently sparked his jealousy. I

31

felt criticized simply for being who I was, when I thought he accepted and loved me.

Rather than staying Big in the moment, I deflated, silent, in the face of his tirade, even though I found his accusations unfair. That night, we split up after two years together, a long time in my young love life, because I perceived no choice in how to relate to him or how to speak up for who I was.

Whenever I saw him over the next year until I graduated, I felt a snap of pain in my chest. I thought about and missed him for years afterward and even tried to contact him unsuccessfully. Since then, I have worked hard to regain my trust and openness in intimate relationships with men.

Today, I'd like to think that I'm more adept at creating choice in how I respond during these types of moments, making decisions appropriate to the situation and the other people involved. Intellectually, I know I always have a choice—both during the moment and afterwards. Still, I am continuing to learn how to have and act on choices during the inconsistent moment.

Similarly, Frank is learning as he goes, too. While polishing the silver to help his neighbor prepare for her daughter's upcoming wedding, he offers to house an out-of-town wedding guest.

"But immediately I thought, how, if my wife did not want to do this, would we ever back out of this? It was not even negotiable. I mean in our neighbor's mind, it was settled. She made a phone call and did not put any caveats on my offer, like 'but my neighbor has to check with his wife, etc.' So that was really very bad." Because he values making joint decisions with his wife, as well as being helpful, he feels trapped in this "very bad" situation.

Strategy Time

During the "I have no choice" moment, you can lose your perspective of the choices you really have available. Take a timeout. And bake a metaphorical cherry pie. I chose cherry because I like it. You can choose your own flavor, if you like. When a pie cools, you then cut it into slices, often eight of them.

Draw a circle on paper, and divide your pie into eight parts by drawing a plus from end-to-end and then a 'x' through the plus. Now, come up with eight options for your current situation. Be sure to include your "I have no choice" option as one of the eight.

Feel free to be wildly impractical in your brainstorming. Asking Hillary Clinton for advice can be one of the options. Creative thinking can help jar loose practical, actionable and desirable choices. One risk when stuck is that you stop listening to your own creative, inner voice.

SUPPRESSING YOUR VOICE

One repercussion of choicelessness is withholding your voice. You may choose not to speak up to prevent disapproval or to preserve a relationship. Angered by workplace injustices, Ben, a social worker, began organizing union activities—a Big moment. Within a month, he left that agency and started a new job.

Asked to work on a holiday in case a client walked in the clinic, which he anticipated would be a waste of time, Ben agreed in order to prevent disapproval. "It didn't make sense. Just like at the old place. But I'm new on the job, and who am I to argue? I do want to present myself as someone who is willing to get along. Agreeing to work seemed easier, because I'm a new employee, and I want to give the impression that I'm flexible and can meet the needs of the place."

Later he acknowledged that no clients came to use their services. Interesting that one person can have such divergent experiences over similar issues so close together in time.

Over-concern for what we deem appropriate in the situation may rob us of our sense of choice, muzzle our voice, and leave us Small when that concern matters more than our values in the moment. Situational pressures can bring out our desire to look good, stemming from what we perceive is appropriate and the 'shoulds' in our life.

Ron, the teacher who was so vocal about the zoo field trip, also faces situations when he holds back. In an attempt to sustain a new romantic interest, when his date made some comments he found offensive, he made a choice.

"If you think black people are inferior, then you're wrong. I have no problems just saying that you're wrong. You're just wrong. But as soon as I heard her make that comment, I didn't even challenge her, because I wanted her to stop talking about it. She isn't going to change her mind.

"Challenging her would be an immediate parting of our friendship. Probably we would never speak to each other again. I thought, well maybe I can prevent that from happening." As you can imagine, the relationship did not last too long after that encounter. Still in that moment, his choice to deny what was intuitively more important left him feeling Small.

Relationships are clearly a dance, with varying degrees of straightforward movements and a few turns and dips. To preserve relationships, you may sometimes find yourself suppressing your full voice. And by not speaking out loud, you can squelch your inner, intuitive voice as well.

STRATEGY TIME

Holding yourself back, whether you withhold your voice or your physical presence, can lead to feeling Small. Take a moment. Recall a Big experience. What was your posture like in that moment? How did your voice sound then?

Notice the differences between your posture and voice now and your posture and voice in the Big moment. Gently shift your posture to Big, and remember to breathe. Breathe in to expand the amount of space you take. Good job! Now, notice if you have your voice back.

AVOIDING CONTACT

Another form of disempowerment comes from avoiding potentially sticky situations and confrontation with others. Unresolved, these situations tend to irritatingly linger like a bad blister.

During my senior year in high school, I was named co-editor of our award-winning, biweekly high school newspaper. My beloved journalism teacher was certain she could help us make this partnership arrangement work. Along with the Managing Editor, we formed a triumvirate leading the journalism staff.

Funny how I don't remember the details of any one conversation. The snapshot I carry in my mind is the look on my co-editor's face when she had to deal with me. She, a pale blonde, wore bright red lipstick. When she talked with me, on her thin lips she also wore a sneer, the top lip practically curling to her nose in what I imagined was disdain.

The Managing Editor, who turned out to be a good friend and a good journalist in her subsequent career, and I compared our experiences of that sneer. The journalism teacher watched from a distance.

In my seemingly laid-back fashion, I let my co-editor take control of content and directing the staff of the paper, while I worked closely with the Managing Editor on style and appearance, sold advertising, and wrote an occasional film review or editorial. In other words, I backed down. I backed off.

I played a finite, win-lose power game with her, with me as the loser. To protect myself from that sneer, I gave up my power and made what I thought was the best of that potentially hostile situation—by avoiding my co-editor altogether.

Unlike my powerful moment in junior high, I have more often responded to the power of others as I did with my co-editor. I very quickly assess the cost of taking someone on and facing the situation with integrity, and often just as quickly decide, "well, it's just not worth it." I certainly cannot blame anyone else for giving up on myself in these situations.

Rather than dealing directly in an uncomfortable moment, the situation can fester based on white lies. Judith, a massage therapist, didn't want to attend a professional development class taught by a friend of her boss. "I said, 'I'm sorry, I can't come right now because something came up.' Now of course, the teacher is asking if I want to come to the next one, next month.

"So I have to decide whether to tell her my real reasons—I'm not sure that this teacher is really somebody that I will learn much from. Because the teacher is a friend of my boss's, it is kind of touchy. So I am feeling pressured by the relationship with my boss.

"I want to go somewhere else, to another state. Just avoid it altogether. I still feel I'm in a very uncomfortable position now." And she knows she will have to deal with it sooner or later. Avoidance may seem like a good strategy in the moment. Yet the situation seems to drag on, with lack of closure, repercussions, guilt and more.

Richard, a project manager, has a non-paying client. Rather than call the client himself to request payment, he asks a sub-contractor to, reasoning if Richard isn't paid, then the sub-contractor won't be paid either.

Recognizing that he's passing-the-buck, he admits, "this is a conversation I don't want to have. It's unpleasant. The subcontractor has placed trust in me. Although he doesn't fully understand it, I am betraying that trust."

Already feeling lousy about his choice, Richard also knows he will take this same course again. "I'm using him to enhance my position. I'm not going to lose sleep over it, and I will do it again."

STRATEGY TIME

Avoiding potential conflict may seem like a good choice in the short run, but typically will not make the issue disappear. Remind yourself that you can push through your discomfort to resolve the situation in a more satisfying way.

Make two lists. First, list what is likely to happen if you continue to avoid contact. Then make a list of the worst things that can happen if you do make contact. Be outrageous. Include the absolute worst possibilities. If you could end up homeless, then list it. Going to an extreme can help you find the more plausible middle ground.

Look at both lists. Which seems more likely? Which choice gets you more of what you want in the long run?

Conflict can be just plain hard to deal with. As one colleague remarked about conflict, "when you avoid situations, then you don't have to deal with what you're going to feel and what you're going to think, because there isn't any thinking or feeling." Not thinking or feeling? Not a very good choice.

DISEMPOWERED COMPLETELY

One of my recent stories combines several of the disempowerment themes. As a mid-career adult, I entered my first doctoral program with some trepidation. During college, I learned that while smart, I was hardly an academic.

So, I started this program already catastrophizing about how all my colleagues would read James Joyce for pleasure and discuss the differences between Marxist and Hegelian philosophy over lunch. Why in the world had this prestigious school, with its pick of candidates, selected me? I mean, I knew how to get along with people, but no one would accuse me of being an intellectual.

Early on, I met one of my cohorts Ken. Terribly bright and funny, he was a delight. While clearly a great intellect, Ken would hardly rub my nose in my own insecurities. I felt such relief!

During our first semester, one seminar was very loosely structured. Whichever direction the leaderless seminar conversation took was just fine with this seminar's professor.

The first week, two other white women and I engaged in what felt to me like a lively conversation on the meaning of community, a topic much in my thoughts at that displaced time. Having moved from a city where I had invested energy in my community for a new city and school, I was reflecting a great deal on what being a member of a community meant to me.

After the class, Ken called me. He said he had spoken with the other two women as well as the seminar's professor. "I've been in other seminars like this in the past," he explained, "where the white women dominate the discussion. Would you be willing to try an experiment?"

Holding my breath, I continued to listen. He continued, "would you be willing to listen instead of talk to make space for the minority voices to enter in?"

Not only did I agree to conduct the experiment, I totally gave my voice away. For the rest of that painful semester, I didn't open my mouth in that seminar and spoke only when I had to in the others. I interpreted what this bright, obviously caring person said to me as meaning I had nothing of value to say. I added shame to my insecurity. Talk about low self-esteem.

I became an observer, rather than an actor, in the theater of that year. No irony that I have no photos from this period. I disappeared. I got lost. I died a little death and became a ghost of myself.

As an observer, I watched Ken interact with faculty, our fellow students, and other students in the program. I realized that he was extraordinarily gifted for making himself pleasing in any situation, just as he had been with me.

Rather than share my experience of his early request, I avoided him. As Anne Lamott says, "there are people out there in the world who almost inspire me to join the government witness protection program, just so I can be sure I will never have to talk to them again." Ken was just such a dangerous person for me.

Two years later, when I decided to leave that program for The Union Institute, I realized I had given myself up for someone else's experiment. Whatever his intention, I interpreted Ken's words in my own insecure, self-critical fashion. Ken hardly ruined my experience in that program. I did. With that a-ha, I responded favorably when Ken asked me to a farewell lunch.

There, I reminded him about his phone call. I told him about my interpretation and resulting action. He seemed genuinely surprised and very apologetic. I told him he was not responsible for my decisions or actions. I really had victimized myself, as I had the power to make different choices, but lacked the awareness, then the courage to do so.

Through my stories, you can see the power I attribute to others, disempowering myself. When disempowered, I feel over-whelmed and stuck, hold myself back and avoid conflict.

The power I shrink from is separate from the power of institu-tions, which have no real meaning for me. People and situations are what influence my responses and ultimate behavior. How I respond to the next powerful person I meet in my life will build on how I acted in junior high, high school and seven years ago. I'll keep you posted.

I AM SMALL WHEN REACTIVE

While some moments capture our attention and call for effort, in other moments, we rely on habit—like being on automatic pilot. Similarly, in many of the Small experiences, we have an imme-diate reaction typified by behavior that is unintentional.

Automatic behavior involves the unconscious and is sponta-neously activated in response to a situation. This behavior often repeats itself and tends to use minimal energy, which is perhaps why we fall into it so easily and build habits around it. Of course, some automatic behavior stabilizes the routines of our life, like driving a car and taking a shower, neither of which requires your full, mindful attention to every hand and foot movement.

The automatic responses that result in Smallness are quite dif-ferent from the simple routines of life. These experiences involve reactions that preclude our best intentions and effective action from shaping our experiences.

CAUGHT OFF GUARD

These situations may not always be calm. After working with a clinic patient for an extended period over the phone, nursing assistant Vicki is caught off guard. "He said something to me that was so sexually vulgar that I threw the phone down, and I ran into my boss's office, and I closed the door, and I cried.

"I'm not the type of person to get real emotional at the drop of a hat. But I was just exhausted. And I thought, how dare you? How dare you do this to me? I was so mad." Priding herself on her gentleness and patience, she lives with embarrassment over her response.

OVERRIDING INTENTION

Sometimes, planning and intention can be thrown out in the face of a reactive response. Different from intuition that guides decisions, automatic behavior can have a habitual routineness about it. Habits tend to override your intentions and resulting behavior. These habits are unconscious, perceived as unchangeable, and act as a barrier to your desired results.

Alice's best intentions about establishing a good relationship with her teenage son gets challenged by her habitual responses. "My son is fourteen and has a mouth on him. He can be disrespectful with his tone of voice or with sassing back.

"We were sitting at the dinner table, and he was getting mouthy. What his exact words were, I don't know. But his last was just a grunt. He insisted it was related to the TV that was on and music he was hearing from that. I think it was directed to me and still feel it was directed to me.

"So I said, 'that's it. You're not going to basketball tonight.' They are in a big tournament. I said, 'you are not going. The CD player, taking that away hasn't worked. Nintendo, taking that away hasn't worked. Grounding you hasn't worked. Maybe taking away your going to the game tonight is strong enough for you to get the message that you need to think before you open up your mouth.'

"I ended up letting him go to the game. He begged me and wouldn't stop. All I could think was just stop, just leave me alone. I just broke down. I said, 'the heck with it, you might as well just go.' So he went. It was his pestering that got on my nerves.

"He didn't even play but about two minutes in the game. That really aggravated me even more. Because we could have stayed home and not made the trip." Her breaking down and giving in is part of how they routinely relate. So regardless of her intentions, habit took over.

READY-FIRE-AIM

Automatic and reactive behavior has a ready-fire-aim quality that can leave you frustrated and disappointed in yourself or the outcome. Effortful processes are more flexible, yet they require enough time and thought to override your spontaneous automatic responses.

Being choiceful in the moment is crucial to allowing an effortful process to take place. In the moments when my first and not my most effective response dominates, I seem doomed to ruminate about how I might have handled myself better if I had just slowed down, considered my intentions and values, and assessed my situation through the panoply of choices that help make me Big.

While in graduate school, I traveled with three other learners to spend a day at the Abbey of Gethsemani in Kentucky. Growing up Jewish, I have had little experience in the practice of Catholicism. So I looked forward to attending a mass at this Abbey, the well-known residing and burial place of Thomas Merton, as well as the other experiences of the day.

Taking lunch at the Abbey involves eating in silence. The four of us arrived at the retreatant dining hall promptly at 12:30 p.m. To my surprise, rather than being enveloped in a silent environment, a loud tape was playing. Seated across from one of my colleagues, I noticed he avoided looking at me, perhaps to prevent any temptation to talk.

Then I began to really notice the tape. The speaker, very intrusive, had a soft southern accent and spoke in a preachy voice. His voice frequently spat fire. My childhood in Texas helped train me to tune out preaching, proselytizing, fire-and-brimstone talk, but all of a sudden, this voice captured my attention.

The derogatory voice referred to the lack of faith of the Jews, demonstrated by rejecting Christ. Up to that point, I hadn't been paying attention to the words, but rather was eating as quickly as I could to leave that uncomfortable environment. Breathless, I glanced at my companion, but he was resolutely staring at his plate. I looked down at my food again, realizing I really hadn't tasted it anyway and had now lost interest.

I began to listen, in an attempt to understand what this detached voice was trying to communicate. I think the speaker was denouncing some group that blames or chastises Jewish people. But I wasn't clear about the point of view.

The tone, volume and insistence of this voice were rattling me. How many of these diners were actually listening? How many were actively trying to understand the framework of the speaker's message, in spite of the tone?

I hastily finished my meal and left the dining room. Another of our group, Joanne, a nun with whom I had traveled from Cleveland, was waiting outside, too. We spoke of trivialities and finished our day at the Abbey before heading to a nearby airport for our return. But by the time we boarded our plane, I was exhausted, more than a little frightened and deeply saddened.

Flying home, I made some allusive comment about the day being somewhat trying. Joanne responded, "for me, too!" She felt "quite devastated and embarrassed" by the tape at lunch. We spent the next several hours of travel together discovering and processing our mutual alienation.

Joanne was concerned not only about my response in particular, but also about the apparent contradiction with the hospitable mission of the Abbey. Gethsemani is the home of Trappist-Cistercian-Benedictine monks. "St. Benedict insisted that his communities show a warm welcome to guests, as though receiving Christ himself. St. Benedict saw this as a basic Christian duty which could only open one for the gift of prayer," quotes the Abbey's literature.

Thomas Merton wrote about the power of genuine love and that wrong thinking inhibits love. What would Merton say about this tape? Where is the love in that voice? The hospitality?

To Joanne, I expressed the horror of hearing the tape during a silent meal in a roomful of people, who seemingly had no response. Not only was I concerned about a perpetuation of hatred toward Jews, something that feels familiar in my life, but also I shared my fears about indoctrination based on ignorance. Put hungry people in a room, prevent them from speaking, then blare out a message. How can our sub/unconscious deny that message? What strength is needed to repel this blaming and shaming?

As a nun, Joanne was concerned that I, in some way, might hold her responsible or that our friendship might be endangered over this experience. Together, we came to see that such pain doesn't linger between people who can reach an understanding through dialogue. I believe that only nameless, faceless voices of institutions cause such destruction.

What I so appreciate about Joanne was that she acknowledged our mutual hurt. We consoled each other, fortified the bridge of understanding between us, and learned the power of individual connection that can overcome institutional oppression. Ultimately, we both wrote of our distressing experiences to the Guest Master of the Abbey, whom we had met after that lunch.

Today, I tell you the story with righteous indignation. Yet as I reflect on the lunch experience, so vitally unpleasant for me, I have also wondered what kept me from simply getting up and walking out or from speaking out loud? Why did I swallow those words in that ugly tone with my warm cheese? What kept me from saying something to the Guest Master when we visited with him? What function did suppressing myself play?

I think that 'the good girl' part of me, that habitual response of putting on a sunshine face, dominated. Rather than making the effort in the moment to take a stand for myself, I retreated behind a mask of appropriateness.

Fortunately, very little time passed before Joanne and I supported each other through this painful experience, and I moved on to take action. Converting from a habitual, automatic response to engaging more effort involved a learning process for me—a process explored more deeply in Chapter 7.

STRATEGY TIME

Converting from Small to Big involves overriding your habitual, reactive and automatic responses with effort. That effort involves checking in with what is important to you—your cherished values and principles. Effort takes time.

The best strategy for these situations is to slow down. Take a time out. Even say "time out" out loud. If you are with other people, change your environment or where you are sitting. If you are seated, stand up. Get a drink of water. Stretch. Breathe. Close your eyes for a moment. Slow down.

Then ask yourself, what is important in this moment? How do I want to be in this moment? What are my choices in this moment?

NEGATIVE SELF-CRITICISM

During Integrity Moments that resolve into Small experiences, we can evaluate ourselves in light of those experiences with regret, guilt, resignation, embarrassment, disgust, hopelessness, disappointment, discomfort, evasion or resentment. We may assess that we have broken some 'shoulds' or social rules.

These stories reveal an 'inner critic' which negatively judge or actively uses critical language, such as 'I should.' In essence, the critic describes, assesses, and critiques your actual behavior. "I would like to think that I am more responsible," laments one self-criticized person.

Other story tellers toss off self-disparaging asides. Notice how often you hear yourself and others make statements like "that makes me feel sort of wormy," "if I really thought about it, then I would be appalled at myself," "I felt really sick about myself," and "normally in society, that's not what you're supposed to say."

Healthy guilt is appropriate as it leads to remorse, but not self-hate. Until, that is, the guilt converts to shame. While men may experience the same feelings, studies show that "basic female shame" is more common. It centers on low self-worth based on unconscious assumptions that others are better.

Many women internalize negative beliefs that play like a broken record: I am not good enough, I can never do enough, I am not worthy. The should-ought refrain also represents a common internal voice.

With low self-esteem and negative self-belief systems, women tend to create the results they unconsciously think they deserve. How useful to remember you become what you perceive. You become what you believe. Positive or less so.

Part of integrity is the relationship to yourself and perceptions you hold about yourself in relationship to your world. Your inconsistent experiences can cause a self-esteem blow or further reinforce a negative self-assessment. For example, after Anne made a mistake at her new job, "I was feeling rejected and inferior, because I knew I wasn't qualified for the job. Then I started getting into a groove, having feelings of rejection. I feel like such a failure."

Breaking the cycle of "feelings of rejection" proved to be a real challenge for her, until she finally left that position and the company. Small experiences can leave little room for anyone else to console or for generosity of spirit.

STRATEGY TIME

One recent Integrity Moment workshop participant described her negative self-talk as a Greek Chorus. However you think of that inner, critical voice that is negatively assessing you during and after the Small moment, you can break its power over you. Listen to the message of this critic. What does this voice want you to know? How can you use this message like advice? Maybe this part intends something positive for you.

If it refuses to be cooperative, refute the critical voice. Tell the negative voice how it is wrong. Collect information that proves it wrong. Question negative assumptions about yourself. Out loud three times daily, say affirmations that positively reinforce who you are and who you are becoming. Say, "I am Big" as one of those affirmations.

Re-discover the part of you that is Big. Invite this part of you and the Small, critical voice to have a conversation. What happens?

Set your metaphorical copy machine on reduce and shrink the critical voice. Focus on what is working and positive, rather than on what is wrong. Find the humor in the situation. The Greek Chorus fades with humor and lightness.

CHOOSING TO BE SMALL TO PRESERVE INTEGRITY

Surprisingly, at times, we may want to escape or avoid Bigness. Perhaps we use this strategy to preserve integrity for ourself or for others. For example, Jan is enthusiastically given a Christmas present of a suit from a second-hand shop by her sister, who is financially strapped.

"So I told her the suit fit fine, even though it didn't. I didn't want to burst her bubble. I feel a little uneasy, because I know I did lie to her. At the same time, I think the ends justified the means in this case. Because she would have been devastated."

Although uncomfortable with her lie, Jan intended to make her sister happy. She identified this moment as an inconsistent experience, which left her feeling Small. Still in the big picture, her choice in this one moment serves her ongoing relationship with her sister, allowing her to be Big overall.

STRATEGY TIME

One strategy for long-term Bigness involves going up the Eiffel Tower to see differently. Pablo Picasso attributed developing his distinctive Cubist style to the newly constructed Eiffel Tower. Once he rode up to its top, he was able to look out, down, around, all in ways new to him. The Eiffel Tower forever changed the way he looked at the world and people in it.

To see your situation with new perspective, go up the Eiffel Tower and ask yourself how this moment fits in with the big picture? Have you seen this circumstance before? How important is this event? Do you want to deal with it now? Look all around the situation. How might someone else see it differently? How might your actions shift in a different setting?

If you are hooked by another person in the situation, can you separate their behavior from who they are? How is their behavior sparked by the situation? That person is as complex as you. Ask yourself, "is this about me?"

If you are caught in your thoughts, think about what you are feeling, or vice versa. Shuttle your ways of knowing. Check in with your intuition.

In case other people are making themselves Big at your expense, remember what Peace Pilgrim learned:

> No outward thing—nothing, nobody from without—can hurt me inside, psychologically. I recognized that I could only be hurt psychologically by my own wrong actions, which I have control over; by my own wrong reactions (they are tricky, but I have control over them too); or by my own inaction in some situations, but like the present world situation, that need action from me. When I recognized that how free I felt! And I just stopped hurting myself. Now someone could do the meanest thing to me and I would feel deep compassion for this out-of-harmony person, this sick person, who is capable of doing mean things. I certainly would not hurt myself by a wrong reaction of bitterness or anger. You have complete control over whether you will be psychologically hurt or not, and anytime you want to, you can stop hurting yourself.

Finally, sometimes simply telling your story to an empathetic listener can help you shift from Small to Big. Own your experiences. You can clear away much of the story's pain and be left with lessons to learn. Tell your stories. I want to hear them!

All the strategies in this chapter are based on the assumption that you want to convert your Small experiences to Big ones. Even if you choose to be Small to preserve your overall integrity, your choices allow you to be Big in the long term, rather than be a victim of circumstance.

Integrity involves a self-perception process

Consistent with Core Values	Inconsistent with Core Values
I am Big	*I am Small*
Active Stance	Disempowered
■ Taking a Stand	■ Feeling Overwhelmed
■ Speaking Out	■ Stuck, Lacking Choice
■ Desire to Influence	■ Suppressing Your Voice
■ Establishing Clear, Firm Boundaries	■ Avoiding Contact
Effortful Behavior	Reactive Behavior
Generosity of Spirit	Negative Self-Criticism
■ Volunteering Time	■ Should-Ought Voice
■ Empathy	■ Inner Critic is Present
■ Teaching/Mentoring	■ Reinforces being Big

I am Big and I am Small create a life space out of which your integrity lives and operates. When you nibble the mushroom and grow Big, you have room for generosity and the time to effortfully create actions that reinforce your Bigness. Speaking out, taking a stand, acknowledging your desire to influence, and setting and holding clear boundaries are all features of being Big.

When you are Small, you fall into disempowerment, shrinking your available space to others to ant-like size. You may criticize yourself quite negatively, as well as react automatically, without employing the effort to be Big.

In my life, I notice a continual balancing of Big and Small experiences, each having quite a different effect on my internal world. Like Alice in Wonderland, I am working to control my size, because after all, I love the full richness of the me that is Big.

Nelson Mandela, in his 1994 Inaugural Speech, cries out:

> *Our deepest fear is not that we are inadequate. Our deepest fear is that we are powerful beyond measure. . . .*

Your playing small does not serve the world. There is nothing enlightened about shrinking so that other people won't feel insecure around you. . . . As we are liberated from our own fear, our presence automatically liberates others.

I trust that you are learning as I am about the power of Bigness and how to shift from being Small to Big. For you can create a good life full of integrity. The world around you desperately needs you to act from your integrity. May your own stories as well as the stories in this book bring you insight, motivation, and hope.

In Chapter 4, we delve further into the dynamics of the Integrity Moment—specifically the values and principles that serve as the core to defining the content of your integrity. But first, reflect on what you have been learning here with the following Personal Application tools.

FURTHER READING

Belenky, M.F., Clinchy, B.M., Goldberger, N.R., & Tarule, J.M. (1986). *Women's Ways of Knowing: The Development of Self, Voice, and Mind.* New York: BasicBooks.

Bepko, C. & Krestan, J. (1990). *Too Good for Her Own Good: Breaking Free from the Burden of Female Responsibility.* New York: Harper & Row, Publishers.

Broom, M.F. & Klein, D.C. (1995). *Power: The Infinite Game.* Amherst, MA: HRD Press, Inc.

Frankl, V.E. (1959). *Man's Search for Meaning.* New York: Pocket Books.

Lamott, A. (1994). *Bird by Bird: Some Instructions on Writing and Life.* New York: Pantheon Books.

Merton, T. (1965). *Love and Living.* New York: Farrar Straus Giroux.

Pilgrim, P. (1982). *Peace Pilgrim: Her Life and Work in Her Own Words.* Santa Fe, NM: Ocean Tree Books.

PERSONAL APPLICATION

Recall a recent experience in which you acted inconsistently with your basic values and principles. Describe it here.

Who was involved?

What were you thinking and feeling?

What did you say and do?

What happened? What was the outcome?

How do the themes of being disempowered fit here?

What other factors were present?

What strategies could help you shift this type of experience to I am Big?

PERSONAL APPLICATION

Invite a friend or loved one you feel very comfortable with to say "beep" every time s/he hears you say the words 'should,' 'ought,' 'must,' and 'need.' These are a clue that your inner critic is present. Substitute the word 'want,' and notice how your experience is affected.

Make some notes here for a week. What do you learn about yourself?

PERSONAL APPLICATION

Recall a recent experience when you were critical of yourself. Note it here. Allow your unconscious to give you a song, image or movement that represents who you were in that moment.

Now remember the touchstone for your generosity of spirit.

Allow the self-critical song, image or movement to transform into your touchstone. Notice the difference in your experience of yourself.

PERSONAL APPLICATION

Write a letter to the part of yourself that can feel disempowered. Is the part also critical? What are the criticisms? Acknowledge the part. Don't fight it. Recognize that the part has a positive intention for you. What is that positive want? Honor this part with your letter.

Now notice your relationship with this part. How has it shifted?

CHAPTER 4

LIFTING THE FOG: RECOGNIZING YOUR VALUES

The moment I arrived at my new home of Portland, OR, I knew I had made a terrible mistake. Fog hung heavy on the trees outside the sliding glass doors leading to my apartment's balcony. That dark heaviness settled on me, too.

From the time the movers delivered my banged up furniture to leaving 18 months later, I lived in the fog of my choice to move there. What had I been thinking? Having completed graduate school, I returned to living in the Northwest almost by rote. Seattle, my home for five years before school, was a place of tremendous growth for me, as I grounded myself in who I was becoming.

For the first time, I lived in a place where the community's value system matched mine. I grew up in a family-friendly Dallas that had grown clean, fast and glitzy. While in my career-oriented 20's, I felt the pressure to drive a nice car, dress up for dinner and wear my success in my lifestyle—none of which was important or interesting to me.

After each intolerably hot summer, I swore it would be my last. Yet year in, year out, I circled the laps of the seasons. Finally, at age 29, I made the break. I decided to move to Seattle, a place I had enjoyed on business travel. I actually knew very little of the place and had only one acquaintance there. But something in Seattle, perhaps the water and soft salty air, was calling me.

During my brother Robert's first visit, he commented, "you belong here. You're such a hippie!" Well, perhaps I was. By being in a place where the value system matched my own, I was able to turn inside and begin developing a life congruent with what was important to me, rather than fighting as a misfit with the world around me.

I filled my life with many forms of beauty: returning to studio dancing, discovering social dance again, serving on a theater board, volunteer ushering at other theaters, writing fiction, attending book readings, exploring my spirituality, hiking, taking day trips to explore the wonders of the area, and making friends. Many friends, for the first time since college, who saw the world as I did. I learned about community.

So after graduate school, I assumed I would return to the Northwest. During the four years I was away, Seattle had grown even more expensive, and as I was starting up my private practice as a Life Coach, I decided to go to Portland instead. I thought Portland would be less expensive, yet provide the same kind of life I knew from Seattle.

Perhaps I had changed. Perhaps Portland is different from Seattle. Perhaps the chemistry between me and the place was sour. Whatever the reason, I had a hard time connecting with people, and those I did become close to moved away. I grew disinterested in exploring the beauties of the place, and unstimulated by the arts offerings.

And the fog. Oh, the fog. When I rented the apartment, sun radiated the place with warmth. That was on a summer's day. For many months, the fog hung on the hillside of that building. Dark and damp did not improve my mood.

When I moved to Washington, DC, and my step lightened and quickened again, I learned something important about my values. I value people over place! Of course, I had known that, but somehow, I needed to live the opposite to realize my priorities. I had so many fantasies of Portland before moving there. I had chosen a place over people.

In Washington, I was immediately welcomed by many different people. During my first week there, I met a woman for lunch, who gave me a ride to the airport the next day—a lovely gesture. During the first month, another woman invited me to her home for a holiday celebration. Others invited me into their discussion

56

salons, women's groups, book clubs and arts groups. I was amazed, touched, delighted. I had found community again.

With exuberance, I explored the cultural and spiritual beauties of Washington, on my own and with new friends. I learned that my value of beauty takes many forms. While I love and appreciate natural beauty, I prefer to live with the beauty of people and community. My values priorities are clear. The fog has lifted.

YOUR CORE VALUES AND PRINCIPLES

My extended Integrity Moment centered on getting the meaning and priority ranking of my core values straight. I learned the difference between living centered on values of lesser importance and the I am Big experience of living aligned with central values.

Now that we've explored the experiences of Big and Small, we can jump into the dynamics of integrity. Why not always be Big? Because our choices in the moment are not always straightforward. To understand how to make the integrity choice involves our deeply held values and principles. What are values and principles? How do you recognize which ones are most important to you so that you can be Big? What do you do when the fog settles in?

DEFINING VALUES AND PRINCIPLES

Principles and values basically refer to the same thing. Each represents your personal cherished beliefs and admirable qualities that provide satisfaction, direction, motivation and meaning to your life.

Personal style and language preferences distinguish values and principles: those who prefer to make decisions using logic and objectivity tend to think in terms of principles; those who prefer subjectivity and empathy frame decision-making in terms of values. (For brevity, I refer to 'values' to represent both.)

Your behavior demonstrates which of your values are active and important in the moment. In fact, you may discover a value or newly realize the importance of another through your very actions, as I did during and after living in Portland.

When your actions fall out of alignment with your values, you may experience fear, guilt, frustration, violation and other emotional imbalances of being Small. These negative feelings can be eliminated by changing your behavior to align with your values or changing your values to align with your behavior. Either choice helps you regain a sense of being true to yourself and being Big.

The Personal Application tools at the end of the chapter help you determine your own top values. When these qualities are present in your life, life is good, you want to jump out of bed to live your day, you feel Big.

ROSE'S STORY

After an arduous job search and a long stretch of unemployment, Rose plunged into her new Human Resources position with a prestigious company with her usual enthusiasm, vigor and hopefulness. Less than a year later, discouraged, stressed and frustrated, Rose is debating leaving the company. What happened?

Rose will tell you that one of her top values is making a contribution. She deeply believed that this new position would allow her to contribute to her new department and consequently the company. Her creativity and talents would spark this contribution.

Although she was recruited to bring new organizational development ideas to her workplace, what she found was a corporate culture deeply entrenched in "doing business as usual." For the first few months, Rose suggested new ways to look at issues, developed alternative methods and designed revisions to programs.

Rose's manager responded by moving her into a more technical area in which Rose had not been trained and really had no interest. To compound the pressure, her duties included technical training of new supervisors. "She told me that's what was really needed and what I was really hired to do," Rose groaned. Then with an edge of anger, she added, "that's not what I remember from the interviews!"

Gradually, Rose's self-confidence started to erode, as she found herself contributing neither her ingenuity nor her competence. "I really didn't feel like I could do anything right." Then, a bit surprisingly, a new twist on her contribution value sprouted. Rose suddenly felt very loyal to the department. She could contribute by being loyal. She would not hear of an internal transfer, much less change companies. Rose wanted to make a difference where she was. She worked hard to shift her attitude to "I can make it work!"

Now, tired and despondent, Rose is anxious for a change, any change. She recognizes that placing the value of loyalty above contribution is not only depressing her, but also doesn't serve her company well. Slowly, she is mobilizing her energy for another job search, both in the company and beyond.

"I know now that this whole mess isn't about me or my skills. I just need to get out and take care of myself. Go someplace where I really *can* make a difference." Rose's shift from Small to Big is beginning, with her value of contribution intact.

VALUES AS LABELS

Naming the value, such as Rose's contribution value, really is a label for an experience. The two of us may share a value label, yet mean something completely different experientially. For example, one dear friend sent me an e-mail expressing her longing to have more fun. I'm so glad I replied by asking what she meant by having fun. "Going out into nature. Getting out of the house," she explained.

For me, fun is any activity or space in which time disappears. And it's one of my top values. My definition is quite different from my friend's, and consequently even as we label the quality 'fun,' value the experience uniquely.

STRATEGY TIME

Find someone you share at least one value with, such as a partner or close friend. Agree on which value you will explore. Take a quiet moment to define for yourself what you mean by the value. How does the other person define it? Now that you have explicitly named your separate meanings, what commonalities and differences show up? Notice your understanding of this person now.

THE VARIABILITY OF VALUES

Values vary across cultures, such as ethnic, racial, and organizational cultures. Values also shift through time in terms of order of importance. This ranking creates a temporary values hierarchy—a prioritized list of core values that motivate you and provide satisfaction. As with Rose, which values are most important for you shift depending upon your situation.

Parents can face values-based dilemmas with their teenagers. Pete, for example, finds his values hierarchy challenged by his teenage daughter. A single parent with custody of Daphne, he has set up house rules to ensure that they get along well and instill some of his top values in his 15 year old daughter.

One of the house rules is to clean up after any meal before heading off for another activity. Since Pete sometimes works the night shift, he and Daphne don't always eat dinner together, so Daphne is often responsible for cleaning up after herself. Pete values responsibility, cleanliness, and orderliness, especially since they live in humid Houston where a sink full of dirty dishes can attract roaches.

Pete also values self-expression, both for himself and Daphne. He wants her to express herself in hair style and clothes. He delights in her playing chess, a game he never mastered, with her boyfriend at a nearby coffeehouse.

But for the past three nights, she has rushed out after dinner to the coffeehouse, leaving the kitchen in disarray. After the first night, Pete talked with her, and Daphne, rolling her eyes and sighing, said, "get a grip, Dad. I have to get there on time!" Frustrated, Pete is gearing up for yet another conversation.

Pete's values have come into conflict, but now he's leaning toward softening a bit on the house rule in favor of Daphne's "wholesome" activity. The situation has led Pete to realign which value is most important. And by compromising on one value, Pete finds himself actually reinforcing his integrity, in terms of strengthening his relationship with his daughter.

We interpret others' behavior in terms of our own deeply held values. This judgment is part of the evaluation you and I make of each other's integrity. Our judgments may leave us closed or less respectful toward others' value systems.

Acknowledging that others may have different value hierarchies from our own can be a big step. Imagine the difference this realization could make in the abortion debate where each side promotes different values. Perhaps you can recall a time when acknowledging the variability of values would have helped you understand another person's actions.

STRATEGY TIME

When you find yourself in a conflict with someone else, take a brief time out. Think about your own values. Which one is charging up your energy? Now, think about the other person involved. What values are motivating this person?

Notice if you experience any shifts with this awareness of the values involved. What new opportunities for negotiation exist? With this understanding, look for strategies and alternatives that help you both emerge Big.

VALUES CHANGE OVER TIME

Since our values are part of our growing, evolving selves, it's no surprise that what we hold most dear in our lives can shift, too. Think back to what motivated you ten years ago. Do those same qualities get you hopping now?

Sometimes how the value gets expressed in your life shifts. As you know, I hold a value of beauty. How beauty is defined in my life has changed over time. Not everyone in our lives knows about these changes though.

Recently, my mother gave me a necklace with antique beads. She knows I used to love wearing vintage jewelry. Although I still admire this style with its beauty and elegance, now I'm working to dispossess in order to simplify my life. I only want to keep items that really mean something to me or suit my current tastes and style. I can admire something beautiful without owning it.

Part of me wanted to quietly accept the necklace. Yet a stronger part spoke out, hoping she would understand my priorities and take the necklace back. Unfortunately, my honesty hurt and confused her. I ended up taking that necklace, which I may never wear, and carefully stowing it away.

Another lesson learned. In my effort to be known by my mother for who I am and what is important to me, I ironically felt Small, both by hurting her and then by taking the necklace after the hurt. Sometimes acting with integrity does hurt other people, as whistle blowers taking a stand against wrongs and leaders of causes such as the Civil Rights movement know.

But this was not one of those times for me. I learned that my relationship with my mother is far more important than expressing to her how my values, and consequently I, have changed. Now I recognize another option—graciously taking the necklace, exclaiming over its beauty, and picking another time to let her know more about me and my values now, perhaps when we are window shopping together.

STRENGTHENING OUR VALUES

Rather than producing conflicts, other situations may reinforce your top values. As a young career woman, Kelly worked as an administrator and found out how solid her values were during a site inspection.

"I noticed in the records that the draperies were cleaned more than necessary. Then when I was inspecting the draperies in about five or six buildings, I noticed that they had shrunk. I was with a person who was in charge of the upkeep and maintenance of the facilities. I said, 'well, look at that. The draperies have shrunk about six inches.' These were massive, huge draperies that went from floor to ceiling."

"He said, 'no, they didn't, they didn't shrink.'

"'Well yeah,' I said, 'we need to complain about the company that's cleaning them. Don't you see that they have shrunk?'

"He said, 'no, you don't understand. The draperies didn't shrink.'

"So it took me about a minute to realize that we were not to level a complaint against this company. In fact, this was all part of a system that was in place in relation to money. We had contracts with cleaning companies that I realized probably involved kickbacks. So, I had to think about what I wanted to do, because it was challenging my own value system. Could I live with that?"

Kelly was then offered new office furniture and decor, which she perceived as a bribe for staying quiet about the drapes. She refused and realized that she was most likely going to change jobs "because I was at odds with a value system and a cultural ethic system that simply was not reflective of my own. I was not allowed to change that, but I just knew that I couldn't function in a healthy way in that environment for a long period of time."

Indeed Kelly was hospitalized with pericarditis from the resulting stress. Even though she suffered physically from her work, she also realized she was Big by sticking to her convictions. In the 25 years since, she learned how resolute her fundamental values are and continues to allow them to guide her decisions.

From Kelly's point of view, she made a Big decision to leave the company. I consider her decision a good one because she discovered and reinforced a bottom line, guiding value for herself, despite the odds presented by her situation. My hunch is that giving in to her situation would have resulted in her being Small.

Know, too, that others may have responded differently in Kelly's situation in order to be Big. Someone else might have chosen to stay and "fight the system" striving to clean it up. That choice would have integrity if it is consistent with their values. How we respond in the Integrity Moment is a reflection of our own values and how we perceive we can enact those values in the moment.

VALUES DILEMMAS

You and I may hold several of the same values, yet with differing levels of importance. As Pete demonstrated above, when a values dilemma arises, internally or with another person, the rank order of those values may not be quite so fixed and clear. Consider Jo's dilemma.

She and I completed a two year training program together. Toward the end, she shared her struggle with me. Jo and one other woman were the only African Americans in the group of fourteen participants. Jo was frustrated by a pattern that she had noticed before with the other black woman.

This woman withheld her own participation in the group and would visibly demonstrate dissatisfaction by alternately sighing loudly and appearing to nap. Often toward the end of each training period, she angrily blurted out her discontent.

The other group participants also noticed this pattern and called her on her behavior. Why was she waiting so late in the process to express herself? This pattern was very disrupting and disturbing for the group.

Jo agreed with the group's confrontation. Yet, as another black woman, she equally wanted to support her colleague. Torn, Jo withdrew into silence, concerned that if she spoke in agreement with the group, she was implicitly criticizing the other woman.

Quite plainly, she was split between her commitment to be loyal to another black woman and her commitment to participate fully in her training program, both values she held very highly. Her solution for that moment was to be silent and also suppress her frustration and anger. She also felt Small.

Can you imagine what you would do in a similar circumstance? Certainly, when it comes to our values, no specific ideal is categorically right or wrong, good or bad. They differ by situation.

STRATEGY TIME

When you're faced with having to choose between two of your deeply held values, take a moment to consider the consequences of the different actions that follow enacting each value plus the consequences of inaction. Perhaps that will make one choice stand out as more desirable.

Ask yourself how you can honor *both* values rather than one or the other. Imagine yourself taking a helicopter ride above the situation, so that you can look down on it with some perspective. What do you notice from up there?

Picture yourself one year from now. You can look back at this moment as history in your life. What did you do, and how do you feel about this moment now that a year has gone by? What advice would you give your younger self?

VALUES AND CONSISTENCY

Acting consistently with our basic values and principles is not always so straightforward. Integrity involves a moment by moment understanding and negotiation of what is important to us, hardly cut-and-dried. Being consistent in our actions itself can be quite a chore. Consistency centers on being the same wherever you are. But how realistic is consistency in practice? You and I could make a game out of naming the different factors affecting the consistency of our identity, values and behavior.

Integrity, in this book, is constructed upon the belief that as part of being human, each of us has both experiences that are consistent with our basic values and principles and those that are not. Because we want more of the former, how do we maintain consistency in a complex, contradictory world?

In reality, inconsistencies are natural. Consistency may even be undesirable. Flexibility and variability are essential for personal development and growth and help us avoid the extremism of rigidity. Ralph Waldo Emerson warns us that "a foolish consistency is the hobgoblin of little minds."

Still, we are concerned about what others think about our inconsistencies. Plus we expect and like consistency and predictability in others' behavior. When people act in unexpected ways, we tend to wonder, what's wrong, why are they acting so out of character?

So, how can consistency over time be possible? Consistency can and does occur in your core, central priorities, such as sticking to your most deeply held values. Consistency with your core values gives an overall impression of consistency. But making your most deeply help values your highest priority may sacrifice a sense of wholeness, if your pursuit of this consistency conflicts with other important parts of your life.

Consider Bob's story. During Desert Storm, Bob was a Lieutenant in an engineering unit of the Army Guard in Tennessee. "My unit was mobilized, and we went to Fort Campbell for transport to Saudi. At that time, they were telling us that we would be gone a minimum of six months and maybe as long as two years. I can't tell you how much I LOVED the Army. If you're sharp, there's no place in the world that you can get the kind of strokes (i.e., ego satisfaction) as the military.

"However, the thought of leaving my wife and two daughters for two years terrified me. I found a loophole that allowed me to get out of going, and I found another Lieutenant who wasn't going who wanted desperately to go. Anyway, I didn't go, but it ruined my career, and they threw me out of the Army. It was the most horrible experience of my life, but I'm firmly convinced that I made the right decision. However, I still have ugly dreams about the experience."

This story clearly demonstrates not only a shifting values hierarchy for Bob, but also the complexities of consistency given the circumstances. In this moment, his inconsistency actually preserved his integrity.

While his value choice for his family was very clear, the pressure and distress of his inconsistency regarding the Army still created internal conflict. But by being inconsistent, the fog lifted, and Bob discovered his most cherished value. Consistency would have called for him to ignore his realization that family was more important than the Army and the tour in Saudi Arabia.

We tend to reconcile our inconsistencies only in the current moment, since our identity continues to grow and develop and our values hierarchies shift depending on the situation. Therefore, the possibility for consistency in the moment versus consistency over time are distinctly different.

While we hope for consistency over time, consistency in the moment is more important for reinforcing our integrity. In order to understand and interpret the Integrity Moment, we focus on consistency or inconsistency between deeply held principles, values, and behavior—in that moment. Otherwise, perhaps having integrity would not even be possible.

VALUES AND COURAGE

Courage may be called for in order to act consistently with your values. Following your integrity may involve taking a stand, often in opposition to another person or idea. When you take that stand, you often learn something important about yourself and your values in that moment.

When Max, who is African American, was a young man in the army, he had a good friend who was white. "One Saturday afternoon, we were off duty. And this guy, who happened to be black and lived on my floor, was creating a ruckus upstairs on the other floor, where my friend bunked. [My friend] talked to him a couple of times and asked him to clear out and go downstairs. He came back up every time, and after a while they got into a fight.

"Some other guys from the outfit who were black were going to jump in to help beat up [my friend]. I grabbed a big stick, like a mop handle or something, and told them not to do it. That somebody was going to hurt real bad if they did. I told them it was between these two guys, and just leave them alone.

"I was ostracized from that point on from any social activities with any of the guys from the outfit who were black. Which I didn't really care about because I knew that what I did was the appropriate thing to do. I mean, the guy had been out of line in the first place. And [my friend] had been nice to him and asked him to clear out and go back to his quarters. And this black guy had been belligerent and nasty, and he precipitated this.

"If [my friend] had been wrong, I wouldn't have acted on his behalf in the way I did. But the fact that the other guy was clearly wrong, that we were friends, and that they were getting ready to gang up on him was not acceptable to me.

"It would have been easier for me not to be in that position. But, I didn't regret my choice. None of them ever spoke to me again. Except for the guy who started the fight. The last day, before we departed, he came up and admitted that he was wrong and apologized. Of course, by then it was too late. I mean, I had already suffered this ostracism."

For Max, the aftermath reinforced the appropriateness of his Big action. This pivotal Integrity Moment helped Max learn what he was willing to take a stand about in his life. By taking a stand, Max also set up a values hierarchy that prioritized "doing the right thing" over inclusion, which has guided his life choices since. Now, Max is an artist and percussionist, "living my own life my own way."

Acting with integrity may not always feel good. Certainly such isolation can be painful. But who knows what role being out of step with the environment plays in supporting innovator's innovations and leaders with strong convictions in making change? Courage is often needed to lift the fog in the Integrity Moment.

THE FOG AND HUMAN FRAILTY

As humans, you and I are messy and even mysterious, perhaps made more so by the varying interpretations of our behavior, our desire to be perceived as consistent, our interest in being well-liked, our striving to determine who we authentically are and the limits to our own self-awareness. Such complexity can shape and affect each of our Integrity Moments.

As the stories in this chapter demonstrate, rarely are our choices in the Integrity Moment easy and straightforward. I believe we're all doing the best we can in each moment given the resources available to us. None of us is intentionally seeking to be Small. So I invite you to honor the good intentions and be gentle with yourself and others as we encounter the challenges in our lives.

Doing our best to resolve these challenges is part of letting the sun shine through the fog so we can be Big. So far, we have been focusing on the dynamics of the Integrity Moment in terms of values complexities. We turn next to considering how who we are effects our choices and actions in the moment.

FURTHER READING

Benjamin, M. (1990). *Splitting the Difference: Compromise and Integrity in Ethics and Politics*. Lawrence: University Press of Kansas.

Emerson, R.W. (1975). Self Reliance. In *Essays: First Series*, pp. 43–90. Boston: Houghton, Mifflin and Company. (Original work published 1841)

Myers, I.B. (1980). *Gifts Differing: Understanding Personality Type*. Palo Alto, CA: CPP Books.

PERSONAL APPLICATION

Determining your core values and principles:
Remember an experience that was deeply satisfying to you. What qualities and aspects of *you* were being honored in that experience?

Think of an experience that was particularly frustrating. List what about you was frustrated and not present in the situation.

Recall a time of deep satisfaction? What made that moment so satisfying?

How about a moment when something very important was going on? What made that moment so important to you?

Notice any repeats and similarities. Clump those qualities together. List your core values and principles here.

Place a check mark next to the one value that is most important to you now.

Put a star next to the value that was most important five years ago.

Do you see how the value that is most important to you can change?

PERSONAL APPLICATION

Now that you have a listing of your core values and principles, recall a time when two or more of these values and principles came into conflict.

What were you thinking and feeling?

What did you say and do?

How did you reconcile the conflict?

What was the new hierarchy (ranked in order of importance) of your values and principles?

What was the outcome?

As you reflect on it now, what comes up for you?

PERSONAL APPLICATION

Imagine how your life would be if you were completely focused on the top priority or one central aspect of your life. How would your life be different? Write a story or a poem about your life filled with this core value. If you prefer, paint, draw or collage your story.

PERSONAL APPLICATION

Acting inconsistently with a value can actually help preserve integrity overall. Remember a time when you were inconsistent and preserved your integrity in that moment. Jot a few notes here to recall the experience vividly.

What did you learn about your values?

What meaning does this experience have in your life now?

CHAPTER 5

YOUR AUTHENTIC SELF

When you get to know someone well, have you noticed how that person's face looks like no other? Bring up a picture of your mother or father in your mind's eye. While you may recognize family resemblances, this person's face would most likely stand out in a crowd for you.

Part of what makes people's faces distinctive is knowing their unique stories, particularly about their Integrity Moments. These stories of being Big and being Small help you know who they are and what's important to them.

Woven inside the unique portrait of our Integrity Moments is our identity and being true to ourselves by acting consistently with that identity. What gives you your unique face? This chapter explores the dynamics of the Integrity Moment of knowing yourself, your identity and your authenticity.

STUDYING OURSELVES

In our culture, a central task each of us faces is to define and know ourselves. The Self is at the center of our psychological universe, and we almost consider knowing ourselves and cultivating our inner nature a duty. So, knowing your self, discovering your identity, becomes a project all its own.

Remember teenager Holden Caulfield in the novel *Catcher in the Rye*? He defined himself by rebelling against the "phony" adult world. So perhaps you spent formative years working on your identity-project. Now, knowing yourself allows you to have more integrity, right?

Not necessarily. Over time, who we are changes, grows, develops, is challenged and even runs amok. And with such continued high value placed on personal growth and self-insight, facing a mid-life crisis—in which your long-held views of who you are may start to crumble—is not uncommon.

Indeed baby boomers are now in mid-life, criticized by some as having achieved their own phoniness. Others have wondered if such a preponderance of mid-life crises even existed before this term became common vernacular. Regardless, many boomers now find themselves refocusing on and even radically redefining who they are and what is important to them.

Further, disparities among parts of ourselves may exist. We may readily recognize that politicians often have a split between their public self, adapting to the demands of the world, and a private self. You might experience different identities, too. Are you the same person at work as in other arenas in your life? So what holds our various parts and identities together?

THE UNIQUE WORLD OF YOUR AUTHENTICITY

Fanny in Jane Austen's *Mansfield Park* says, "we all have a better guide in ourselves, if we attend to it, than any other person can be." So what is this inside-out guide? That inside place, unique for each of us, is our authenticity.

According to Charles Taylor, your original way of being human—or what makes you uniquely you—is your authenticity. Authenticity is comprised of the sum of your life experiences, the meaning you make of those experiences, and your values, attitudes, beliefs and principles. Authenticity incorporates your identity or identities, including all the views of who you are. It collects your Big and Small moments, too.

The uniqueness of your authenticity is created and grows through your interactions and your interpretations of those experiences. So authenticity is not static. It develops and changes throughout life, just as your integrity does.

You may experience your authenticity as an acorn kernel of an oak tree or core fire burning inside. You may hear an inner voice, which, with your attention, becomes increasingly clearer. Listening within helps you to discover and act according to your authenticity and to take charge of and responsibility for yourself.

When I received her letter, Antoinette had just separated from her husband. She wrote, "you asked me if I'm happy. I feel as though I finally had the guts to take charge of my life. Life is opening up again. I have friends, and I even see the glimmer of an intellectual life—kind of like a pilot light. Instead of supporting someone else's intellect, I can really take responsibility for the use of my own time, my selection of friends. I can even see the beginnings of a spiritual life.

"I am finally the architect of my own life. I've bought off on a whole series of mass produced plans for my life without considering, *really*, what works for me—not how it looks or feels to others. Not what I *should* feel but how I really feel. It's hard, scary and wonderful to select the foundation stones myself—but how exciting.

"Since I have no plans to guide me but my own observation, judgment, trial and error, I'll make mistakes—but at least they'll be my own." Her letter continues, "what's different is, how I feel depends upon how I see the situation. I get to choose and decide."

Antoinette is now leading with her Authentic Self, rather than bowing to external pressures or imitating others. Developing awareness of your Authentic Self supports acting with integrity. By knowing who you are and what's important to you from the inside out, you increase your opportunities for being Big.

STRATEGY TIME

If you find yourself being buffeted by the expectations of others, take heart. We deeply value the goodwill and good opinion of others. That said, you can more easily attain the respect of others by putting your authentic self into the world.

If this action is new for you, practice. What's your weakness in giving up your authenticity? Is it saying "yes" to everyone else's needs and wants? If so, practice saying "no" even to little things. "No, I don't want to go to that movie. Let's go to this one." "Now is not a good time to talk. Let me call you back."

By practicing leading with your authenticity, others get to know you for who you uniquely are. And you're the person we want to be in relationship with, not someone who tries to mirror us.

FINDING MY AUTHENTIC SELF

I took several years to find and then put my Authentic Self out into the world. During the transitional period of my life which I described in Chapter 1, I rumbled around, none too gracefully, trying to make a career change out of marketing. While I had loved the early years of that creative profession, I grew into positions of increasing managerial, political and administrative responsibility, which were much less appealing for me.

I discovered Organizational Development through the back door when working with one of my marketing consulting clients, a regional ice cream company. With them, I was able to suggest employee-oriented change strategies, as well as marketing plans. Intrigued, I set out to learn all about this profession.

What attracted me was the opportunity to focus on people rather than things. Now, I was thinking about how to optimize people's lives in organizations rather than getting them to buy my company's products. After a few years of bumbling around, learning and experimenting, I decided to ground myself in the profession by going back to school.

One of my goals for going to graduate school in mid-career was to become clear about who I was as a professional and what I stood for. In short, I wanted to figure out my new career identity and who I authentically was in terms of work.

What I did not anticipate was that going back to school would kick up my own insecurities about who I was as well. Unsure of my academic abilities and overwhelmed by the amount of work involved, I sunk into despair and formed alliances with other students around my pain.

During that time, I continued to consult in Organizational Development. One project involved interviewing people across the U.S. about their experiences working in teams. What struck me was realizing how deeply engaged, indeed mesmerized, I was by people's stories. Our one-on-one conversations led people to make changes they had been longing to enact. They got into action.

Upon reflection, I realized that I have a gift, part of my Authentic Self, for listening to people's stories, hearing what they really want, and helping them commit to the choices that will make that happen. Using this gift energizes rather than drains me as so much of my previous work had.

With that discovery, I realized I was not in the best graduate program for developing my gifts. I switched programs and learned another authenticity lesson. Authenticity also includes the notion of self-authorship. As self-author, we are responsible for making and shaping our own life experiences.

While in my first graduate program, I realized how I authored my experience to be stressful, difficult, even traumatic. I developed the identity of a rebel and malcontent. I operated from a victim stance, blaming the cruel academic world for my problems, and in the process, ruined my chances for happiness in that program.

Later, when I transferred to a non-traditional school that featured self-designed programs, I watched other people repeat my mistake. I couldn't get over how people would choose to create hostile situations for themselves in a program that is self-designed.

Once I discovered my own actions through the mirror of others, I was determined to shift my experience to be more in alignment with what was important to me and author a joyful academic pursuit of my path in life. My identity shifted accordingly, and I regained my integrity by being true to myself. Happily, over this four year period, I shifted from being Small to being Big. As self-author, we choose how we encounter ourselves and our world.

With these life lessons, I touched my Authentic Self, which not only includes the part which is not self-responsible, but also the part that self-sabotages. I resolved this extended Integrity Moment by completing graduate school in a satisfying way and kicking off my new identity as a Life Coach.

STRATEGY TIME

Pay attention to the mirrors that show up in your life. Notice when a friend or colleague is wrestling with an issue that seems really familiar. What can you learn from their life lessons?

Sometimes personal space serves as a mirror of our Authentic Self. Notice where in your home you feel most at home. What makes this space so comfortable? Chances are you have authentically represented yourself here. How can you expand your authenticity throughout your home?

FEATURES OF YOUR AUTHENTICITY

Your Integrity Moments make memorable markers on the face of your life. These marker moments, which have helped define who you are, can be influenced by qualities that comprise your life themes. As you build awareness of your personal patterns, as with distinct and recognizable facial features, you can more easily recognize and navigate your way through new Integrity Moments as they arise.

What happens during and after the Integrity Moment connects you to your personal truth and helps you know what's important to you. What patterns and themes emerge from your history of Integrity Moments?

EARLY STORIES

Sometimes our earliest Integrity Moments are the most formative in shaping our identities. Think back to the earliest Integrity Moment you can remember. Did it resolve as a Big moment?

Kelly, an African American woman who is now president of a large city's community college system, grew up in a small town. She learned something important about her identity and her values, in a childhood Integrity Moment that recounts her first experience of racism.

"I lived in a racially mixed neighborhood and had a friend who was white. I remember playing together, our families living side by side, and our fathers working in the same occupation. At that time, there were segregated schools, so we went to different schools.

"I remember walking to the little downtown area of town one day, and my friend walking faster and faster as we got closer to the town. I remember not understanding why. It was like she was leading me. Then she was literally far ahead of me.

"At first, I was moving faster to keep up with her, and then I didn't. I'm not sure when or why I didn't keep the pace up. We both got what we went for at the store. As we were leaving and walking back home, she was slowing down and waiting for me to catch up so we would end up walking home together.

"I remembered thinking, that was very strange, that was odd. I can't remember now at the point, whether I was told, or whether I figured it out. She had probably been told by her family that it was not advantageous for her to be seen with an African American friend. That it was okay in the neighborhood, but not in the bigger environment in the town. So she was disassociating herself, not because of the friendship, but because of these racial feelings.

"That was a very big turning point for me. I had to decide how I was going to handle that. How was I going to internalize it? Because I had to do something with it. I couldn't just dismiss it. I had to deal with racial issues, friendship. How do you reconcile that?

"I guess I must have understood her choice and somehow separated her choice from who she was. I'm not sure that I was sophisticated enough then to understand how I separated it. But I think I must have understood that somehow, for her survival, her family's survival in terms of their place in the community, that it was a decision she had to make.

"I don't remember being resentful. I remember being less trusting, being less engaged or as open to the friendship. We continued to be friends. And the next time we were going to town, I said, 'you go ahead. I will probably go later.' But I never remember going back to town together. I never remember myself agreeing to do that again."

Clearly, Kelly demonstrated a wisdom beyond her years in understanding her own and her friend's dilemma. Reflecting on the experience, she states, "I think I was an old person as a young kid. I had this knowing. I tuned into my inner voice. Like that older person inside of me who's taking care of me."

I can only imagine the heart-breaking pain, loneliness and confusion that little girl experienced when losing trust and ultimately her friend. The wise Authentic Self guiding Kelly gave her a deep sense that some battles she cannot fight and win.

Perhaps you would have acted differently in that moment. Perhaps you would have talked with the other little girl. Integrity Moments often suggest a myriad of responses, a panoply of options, that we each may resolve differently. The choice the young girl Kelly made was the one that made sense for her at the time and has consequently influenced all of her subsequent life.

PIVOTAL PERSON

Certain Integrity Moments are especially ripe for influence by a pivotal person, someone who can help you define and maintain your integrity. This person may be a mentor, advisor, role model or even a person who enters your life fleetingly, but is especially memorable.

Think back to your Integrity Moments, especially the early ones and moments during transitions in your life. Pivotal people are often influential during these times. The pivotal person inspires you by highlighting a particular path, making a course of action perfectly clear, or by changing your way of thinking and feeling.

My mother once told me she guided key decisions in my early life with an "invisible hand." She helped me begin a life-long study of dance as a child, choose a career development high school, decide to take my first job in a department store and select my college. What seems remarkable to me even today is that I have no recollection of her guidance. I had thought I made all those decisions on my own.

When your values are not clear or a decision is fuzzy, a pivotal person can make a big difference. Wolfe faced a choice point in high school, when he received some strong advice in an unexpected place. While having his eyes examined, he talked with the optometrist, a family friend, about going to college.

"I had very little input from my parents, especially Father, in terms of what to become. I always knew that I would go to college. [The optometrist], someone I really respected, and I had a conversation. I said that I was going to go to Teacher's College, and I didn't really know what I wanted to be. I thought I wanted to be a teacher.

"Anyway, his comment was very short and succinct, and I will never forget it. He said, 'look, you get your ass down to Iowa State. You can become a teacher any time you want to. But you need to get down there where you will get the best education you can get.'

"I will never forget that. He sort of kicked me in the rear to a higher level of education. As it turns out, it was probably one of the most important decisions I ever made, because I went to Iowa State, started in science, switched to civil engineering, and ultimately became an architect and an engineer."

With little family input, this young man had been close to selling his potential short. With key advice during his Integrity Moment, he instead forged his identity by choosing to get the best education available to him and reinforced his own value of maximizing his own potential. The pivotal person actually turned the direction of his life.

SELF-RELIANCE

At different times in your life, you also want to be independent. This self-reliance empowers you to author your own experiences with a kind of enlightened self-interest, to create your identity, and to have a sense of I am Big.

Learning about who we are and what is important to us often involves going out and trying to do things on our own, in our own way. Sometimes this self-reliance means bucking popular beliefs and methods.

Raised on a mid-western farm, Wolfe watched his father struggle with "old ways" of farming. "He even seemed intimidated by some new equipment." Standing in a field, helping his father with the equipment, he discovered his father's fallibility.

Perhaps for the first time, recognizing that he was different from his father, Wolfe resolved to look for the simplest, and therefore best, solutions to any problem. He learned something important about himself in opposition to this important model in his life. Wolfe was starting to become his own person. And now, at 51 years old, he recognizes the importance of this early Integrity Moment for helping him trust his own inner guidance.

STRATEGY TIME

We all have moments in which we need to be independent, solely responsible, self-reliant, and self-interested to follow our own vision and integrity. Other times, when the timing is ripe, we are open to influence, feedback and guidance by others. These factors guide our choices in the Integrity Moment, which in turn help define our identity.

When you're facing an Integrity Moment, think about what is going to be most supportive for you to resolve the moment as I am Big. Who can mentor and guide you in a meaningful way? Perhaps you know someone or have a personal coach who can help you get clear.

If being with a pivotal person is all wrong, you will know it. Listen to your Authentic Self's voice. If it's saying, "no way, I know best!" follow that advice.

Notice the consequences of your choices. What happened as a result? How does the face of your integrity look? What features stand out? Look to the Personal Application tools below to explore further. Then, in Chapter 6, we turn our attention to what happens when the Authentic Self goes out into the world.

FURTHER READING

Austen, J. (1966 edition). *Mansfield Park*. Baltimore: Penguin Books Inc.

Baumeister, R.F. (1986). *Identity: Cultural Change and the Struggle for Self*. New York: Oxford University Press.

Emerson, R.W. (1975). Self Reliance. In *Essays: First Series*, pp. 43–90. Boston: Houghton, Mifflin and Company. (Original work published 1841)

Jamison, K. (1984). *The Nibble Theory and the Kernel of Power: A Book about Leadership, Self-Empowerment, and Personal Growth*. New York: Paulist Press.

Salinger, J.D. (1951). *Catcher in the Rye*. Boston: Little Brown.

Taylor, C. (1991). The Ethics of Authenticity. Cambridge, MA: Harvard University Press.

PERSONAL APPLICATION

Take a moment and reflect on your special and unique authenticity. Invite your Authentic Self forward. Write a letter from this part, giving it a voice, completely introducing itself to you. Alternatively, draw, paint or construct a collage of your Authentic Self.

PERSONAL APPLICATION

Reflect now on the moments in your life that involved acting consistently with your core values and principles. They may have been small moments or they may have extended over a period of time, turning points or everyday moments.

Draw a lifeline with your Integrity Moments marked chronologically on the line. You can use this drawing to support your reflections as you proceed through the book.

What themes and patterns do you notice? In the future, these can serve as your own personal clues that an Integrity Moment is happening.

PERSONAL APPLICATION

List moments when you were influenced by a pivotal person—someone who provided key advice, sparked an a-ha, or served as a role model.

What did you learn about yourself during these moments?

Now remember times when what mattered most to you was forging your own path and doing it your own way, without input by others.

What did you learn about yourself during these moments?

CHAPTER 6

NEGOTIATING THE SITUATION

S ince integrity is about knowing your Authentic Self and what's important, motivating and fulfilling to you, why not have integrity all the time? The simple answer is because you don't live in a vacuum.

Inherently, integrity is a social phenomenon that involves behavior and our interpretations of that behavior. Your actions are potentially shifted, tempered, measured, and evaluated by others and the situations you face. So we now introduce the complexities of the social world into our growing understanding of the Integrity Moment.

The factors effecting your resolution of the Integrity Moment include not only the uniqueness and particularity of who you are, but also the complexities of the situation you face. Some theorists argue that integrity requires remaining resolute despite the situation. I suggest that striving for this unflappable behavior is unrealistic.

Not that we categorically bend to the situation, but rather we operate in groups, communities and societies for which we have a primal need to be a part, to belong. To disregard the influence of the world is the stuff of fairy tales at best and socio-pathology at worst. So while having integrity despite circumstances is admirable, this goal often induces guilt and does not represent the whole picture of the Integrity Moment.

PERSON AND SITUATION

Social psychologist Kurt Lewin said that without considering the environment and its effect on our actions, we cannot fully understand the dynamics of behavior. Individual behavior, then, is a function of both the person and the situation faced.

Integrity combines the freedom to be yourself and responsibility to others and your world. This combination is the result of an ongoing negotiation that seeks to balance your identity—as the authentic, distinctive expression of your self, your words, and your actions—and your assessment of what's appropriate for the situation.

For example, while recently dealing with deadline pressure, I was working with an administrative person. She was abrupt with me over the phone and sent me a fax that was full of typos. This woman challenged my patience. Upset and irritated, I considered contacting her boss to complain. Instead, I decided to wait a day and try again.

By waiting, I learned more about her situation. What I didn't know was that she was new on the job, was feeling pressured by a conference deadline and nagging phones she was responsible for. She was also struggling with a computer program that was new to her. Perhaps her integrity was challenged by the pressures she faced.

I know my own value of harmony in relationships was tested when I thought she was treating me rudely and unfairly. But rather than act hastily, I followed my intuition to slow down and cool off. By learning about her particular situation, I found renewed patience and the opportunity to repair my feelings about her. And the work got done just fine.

Your integrity, then, is an action that involves the complex interplay between you and a particular situation. Understanding that your behavior is affected by both the particular situation and your identity can help you understand how integrity is not a fixed, invulnerable trait. Your overall integrity can be reinforced, grown or challenged by each new Integrity Moment.

While you may long to transcend the uncertainties presented by your environment in order to achieve some sort of universal ideal of integrity, this yearning is wishful unreality. Change, after all, is inevitable. Whether your environment changes or you as a person shift, you can count on it.

Because of changing situations and your own uniqueness as a person, creating a standard set of rules for ensuring integrity is not possible. As much as you may want one, a booster shot for integrity—one that guarantees a life filled with it—is just not feasible.

OUR ENVIRONMENT AFFECTS OUR IDENTITY

Change the environment, and behavior may look totally different. When I started college, I felt liberated from the twelve years of schooling in which I had been dubbed shy, brainy and unpopular. Just by changing environments, I emerged as outgoing and very popular among that brainy crowd.

Bob, who in Chapter 4 chose his family over Army service, tells another story that typifies the importance of environment and our response to it. He describes himself as an "otherwise gentle father who loses his cool at his daughter's baseball games, repeatedly, which is embarrassing (pointing out ass in the word)." A few years ago, his oldest daughter entered a very competitive youth softball league.

"There's a lot of college scholarship money available, and it's very serious ('serious as a heart attack', as we say in the South). Anyway, as the head coach, I was getting out-maneuvered by other coaches as they 'worked' the umpires, the fans, the players, etc. They were winning all the arguments and intimidating me and my players. Out of self-defense I became more assertive. And it worked! When someone got in my face, I got in their's. It was serious, but in a way it wasn't, because it was just part of the game."

Bob goes on to describe his next challenge. "Behavior that's acceptable in one context isn't in another. My youngest plays in another league. There, I'm a fish out of water. This is a 'fun' league where the girls call the 'dugout' the 'dressing room' and their 'uniforms' are 'costumes'. So, what I have to do is figure out how to switch gears."

He has to learn to be flexible in his behavior depending on which daughter he's supporting. For his younger daughter, Bob can calm down, breathe, and enjoy the social aspects of play versus the hard-charging, all-out-to-win league of his competitive daughter. The rules of conduct change with Bob's environments.

OUR IDENTITY AFFECTS OUR INTERPRETATIONS OF BEHAVIOR

Not only do changing situations challenge our dream for an integrity booster shot, so do our variable temperaments and dispositions. The same environment or situation is not seen the same way by all the people involved in it.

In the classic Japanese film *Rashomon*, one event, a rape-murder, is told and retold by each person involved, in an attempt to get at the "Truth" of the occurrence. The stories were so different that at first, I thought they were unrelated. Only later, did I recognize the "rashomon," the term that now describes how each of us can perceive the same event in a different way.

Not only do we perceive events in our own unique way, but we also recognize, interpret and place value on others' integrity or its momentary absence. The rules for evaluating each other's behavior originate in our social world, which we turn our attention to next.

Acting with Integrity

Integrity is a behavior that involves a negotiation between you and your environment

You	+	Your Environment
Knowing your self		Context and situation
Personality and temperament		Place and time
Identity		Others involved
Authenticity		Shift settings to change
Values and principles		points of view

Sorry, there's no booster shot for integrity!

THE SOCIAL WORLD

Part of understanding and interpreting the situation we face involves recognizing how to behave in an acceptable manner. Since we all have a basic, primal need to feel a part of a valued group, the rules for what is acceptable ensure our inclusion and comprise the social world of ethics, morality and virtue.

Indeed, we all have an understanding of these rules, like an internal codebook. In our culture, we live by a basic ethic of the Golden Rule—do unto others as you would have them do unto you. Without the parameters of the social world, you might argue that terrorists bombers have integrity because their actions follow their deeply held values and principles.

Consequently, the social world greatly effects the choices you make during an Integrity Moment. The religious, spiritual and philosophical traditions of ethics, morality and virtue address how we lead our lives and how we want to be in the world. They also suggest how to be a good citizen of our community.

The rules of the social world are pervasive, though sometimes complex and hidden, and represent deeply held beliefs about the nature of the world and our place in it. These rules can be very comforting and provide a stable base for initiating the actions of our lives.

At times, the rules of the social world can also be ambiguous, hypocritical and even immoral. Leaders like Martin Luther King and Malcolm X inspired us to question racial injustices, assumptions behind these social rules and our resulting behavior. By going against the cultural standards, change can happen.

A STORY OF THE SOCIAL WORLD AND INTEGRITY

The novel *To Build a Ship* recounts the experiences of a hermit-like group of white men settling in the coastal region of the Oregon Territory. Living peacefully with their Native American neighbors, the band of men comes together during a crisis.

The captain of their supply ship, travelling from the northeastern U.S., has died, and the men have decided to build their own ship to take its place. One of their company, Sam, has some shipbuilding experience and assumes leadership. Soon thereafter, he literally becomes crazy with love for an Indian girl who already has an Indian boyfriend. Sam falsely accuses the boy of a crime, for which Ben serves as the boy's alibi.

News of the accusation travels and a vigilante group from a nearby settlement forms, vowing to hang the Indian boy for his supposed crime. In the confrontation, Indians and whites alike all tensely wait to see if Ben will step forward and offer the truth of the boy's innocence.

But Sam whispers to Ben that if he speaks out, Sam will leave and abandon the building of the ship, threatening the ability of the men to continue living in the region. After a pressured pause, Ben faces the vigilante group. Rather than provide the alibi for the boy, Ben states he doesn't remember what happened.

Stunned, while reading, I slammed the book shut. Ben has just condemned the innocent boy to die!

Ben justifies his decision. "At that moment the thing that was strongest in my mind was the Ship. We had to finish the Ship, and it made my own guilt petty, trivial. The only thing that was real was the Ship."

In this Integrity Moment, Ben chooses the social world to help him make his decision. The ethics of this group of men suggest to him that completing the supply ship was more important than the sacrifices of any one person. Indeed racial prejudices of the era supported his decision to place the good of the group over the life of an Indian boy. Building the ship became the essential good.

Ben is left with all the repercussions of his choice, both positive and negative. Many other choices were available to him, including listening to another inner voice that recalled his friendship with the Indian boy and his innocence. No matter what you and I might choose, in this moment, Ben's choice is determined by his social world. His choice is the result of an in-the-moment negotiation.

THE SHADOW SIDE OF THE SOCIAL WORLD

When reflecting on how to distinguish the rules of the social world and our individual experience of integrity, I had an important realization. At first, I placed a judgment on the social world as being not only external in formation and influence, but also restrictive, somehow impeding my true self-expression.

I was very focused on the negative, constraining, shadow side of the social world and indeed how many of us respond to these rules with guilt, shame and inner criticism questioning our own worthiness. I became angry about the word 'should' which for me represented the darker aspects of our moral culture.

After many conversations and much study, I realize how important ethics and morality are for providing stability, a sense of safety and belonging, as well as coherence for our community. While dwelling only on the dark side of the social world, I missed the almost invisible strength these structures provide.

As with our famous Civil Rights leaders, we each have the opportunity to rely upon the support of the social world and to question and challenge it, as well. With that realization, I think of the national monuments in Washington, D.C.

Each serves as a metaphor for our country's stability and principles. Yet protests on the Mall are almost a daily occurrence. Being a member of our community does not preclude using our voice to create a better social world.

NEGOTIATING DURING THE INTEGRITY MOMENT

Imagine yourself sitting on the steps of the Lincoln Memorial. Behind you is the grand monument, with its stately columns and classic architectural features. In front of you is the Reflecting Pool. The Mall is busy, and people are moving around you, up the stairs and down.

Here is a place you can contemplate who you are—as a member of our society, represented by this magnificent building, and as a person, mirrored back to you in the Reflecting Pool. What ideals are most important to you? For what will you take a stand? Who are you as a member of your community?

Integrity serves as meeting place on the steps between the Lincoln Memorial and the Reflecting Pool. Integrity represents a joining between the 'me' you authentically are and the 'me-in-community' of the social world.

Your ability to act with integrity is determined by who you are and the specific situation you face. You might be tempted to experience the social world you and the authentic you as different, as in the public and private self split described in Chapter 5. The Prayer for Wholeness recommends otherwise:

We have separated our inner and outer lives
until we no longer see the connection between them.
We have two voices, when there is really only one.
We mistakenly think we must choose between
going out into the world and coming back to ourselves
(Anonymous).

Instead, during the Integrity Moment, some negotiation between the outer, social world and your inner world occurs. If you can imagine a boundary, a movable boundary, between these worlds, integrity sits on that boundary.

The boundary itself may create tension, if your outer and inner worlds collide. The amount of tension varies depending on the situation, the meaning you make of the event, and how you work to incorporate and balance your inner and outer lives. These are the dynamics of the Integrity Moment.

SOME NEGOTIATION STORIES

My friend Dan has an ongoing Integrity Moment, wrestling with himself at the boundary between his outer self and his inner self. Over twenty years ago, he gave up a fledgling acting career for an entry level corporate position. Now, he holds a senior level position, complete with title, status, benefits and

96

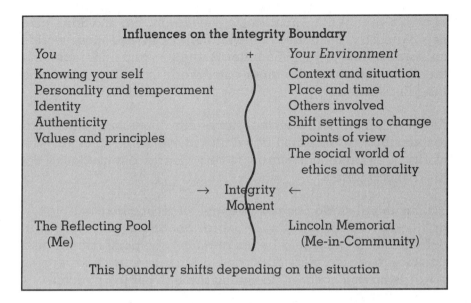

Influences on the Integrity Boundary

You	+	*Your Environment*
Knowing your self		Context and situation
Personality and temperament		Place and time
Identity		Others involved
Authenticity		Shift settings to change
Values and principles		points of view
		The social world of
		ethics and morality
	→ Integrity ←	
	Moment	
The Reflecting Pool		Lincoln Memorial
(Me)		(Me-in-Community)

This boundary shifts depending on the situation

income. Recently, he and his wife purchased a larger home, which they have now contracted out for expensive remodeling. He also regularly saves for his two children's college education.

Despite these outer trappings of success, Dan is deeply frustrated with his work and longs to express himself creatively in a way he hasn't in twenty years. He feels trapped by the lifestyle he and his family have created.

The temptation of the status quo, what seems appropriate for the situation, and just plain comfort lure Dan to stay with his unsatisfying work. His authentic self is urging change and rebellion against self-sacrifice. He resents putting his life on hold, but placates this part of himself by flushing out creative projects at work. "I guess that's just the way things are," he concludes.

In other situations, other Integrity Moments, the drive for authenticity may be resolute. Sara and Jim face a similar situation to Dan. "I think I've just outgrown my work," says Sara. Both have committed to simplifying their lives, cutting down on expenses and becoming very clear about what is most satisfying.

"Yes, we're ready to make some sacrifices," Jim explains. "I expect by the end of the year, we'll both be doing something very different. What, I don't know," he laughs. Jim and Sara have negotiated the boundary between their outer and inner worlds and are leaning toward the latter. Assessing and understanding the complexities at this inner-outer world boundary forms the Integrity Moment.

Al tells a very different kind of story—one of personal and social responsibility. Concerned about global overpopulation, Al, who works in international affairs, is very clear about his desire not to have children.

Yet, his moral stand poses a dilemma of reconciling two 'right's' or 'good's'. He recognizes the moral goodness of raising children. He feels pressured by his parents, who point out he's in a position to raise well-educated children. Our culture also rewards having children, including through our tax structure.

"Even though I'm very clear about what I want to do, I feel squeezed by all these pressures. Like two cement walls closing in on me."

He and his partner Deborah continue to discuss the moral implications, as well as their personal convictions, that will ultimately influence their decision as a couple. "Deborah really respects how I feel, which is great. She is great! But I know she'd like to have a baby, which isn't making this any easier. And now she's worried that if we decide to have kids, she may not be able to get pregnant. The idea of fertility drugs really sends me out the roof!"

The pressures Al and Deborah face reflect that both choices are good ones. Following the conventions of our social world and following strong personal beliefs—neither is bad. Think about how you might advise this couple. What would you do in their situation?

STRATEGY TIME

When you are negotiating the boundary between your personal and social worlds, begin by considering the two different directions. Do you interpret either choice as 'bad'? Do you have any 'should's' operating?

Without trying to change your beliefs, just notice them. Get curious about the origin of your beliefs. Who might have said something like this belief to you? Is it really your belief or theirs? Whatever you notice is great.

Remember your helicopter? Climb aboard. What does flying above the situation add to your observations? What will you be thinking about this dilemma a year after it has been resolved?

NEGOTIATING DYNAMICS

During the Integrity Moment, your personal sense of integrity is at stake. Who you are and what's important to you is being challenged. You may find yourself balancing, indeed negotiating, a boundary between the authentic world of you from the inside-out and the social world of you-in-community.

Resolving the tension at the boundary leaves you with a sense of being Big or being Small in that moment. Take some time now with the Personal Application tools to consider how you negotiate the boundary in your Integrity Moments. Then turn to Chapter 7 to explore the aftermath of resolving these moments.

FURTHER READING AND VIEWING

Badaracco, J.L. (1997). *Defining Moments: When Managers Must Choose Between Right and Right.* Boston: Harvard Business School Press.

Berry, D. (1963). *To Build a Ship.* New York: The Viking Press.

Hitt, W.D. (1990). *Ethics and Leadership: Putting Theory into Practice.* Columbus: Battelle Press.

Rashomon (1951). Embassy Home Entertainment. Los Angeles: Janus Film Collection, 1986.

PERSONAL APPLICATION

To understand integrity, consider both the person involved and the situation at hand. Think of a time when you questioned the integrity of another person.

What effect does considering the situation have?

How has your interpretation of the outcome shifted?

Recall a time when you have questioned your own integrity.

What effect does considering the situation have on your assessment?

How has your interpretation of the outcome shifted?

PERSONAL APPLICATION

Write yourself a letter. What does it mean to be true to yourself in terms of your authenticity? What does it mean to be true to yourself in terms of your ethics?

Perhaps you've now discovered an Authentic Self and an Ethical Self within. What do these parts have to say to each other? Try writing their responses as a dialogue.

PERSONAL APPLICATION

Describe a recent experience that posed a dilemma at the boundary of your personal and social worlds.

What did your Authentic Self call for?

What did your Ethical Self want?

How did you negotiate the boundary between the two? What are your thoughts and feelings about that now?

Knowing what you know now, how would you negotiate the boundary?

CHAPTER 7

LEARNING FROM THE INTEGRITY MOMENT

The large, oblong photo album, heavy with pages and years, presses down on my lap. Each page carries the mysteries of a life I hardly remember.

"You were so cute." Mom caresses one photo with an arthritic finger.

For hours, she and I go through each book—red-covered for Robert; blue for Marty; her own book, capturing my parents' early married years, green. Mine is plain beige and like the others, tattered around the edges.

My trips to Dallas to visit family almost always involve poignant expeditions to the photo albums. So many people to know. My father is one of ten children, and I want to remember them all.

"That's Sarah."

"No, that's Miriam," Mom clarifies.

"Can't be," I insist.

"Well, it is."

I ooh in amazement at the uncanny resemblance of my mother's mother, sister and niece. My mother, a beauty in her youth, shows me the glamour pictures she sent to boyfriends during World War II. "Two of them died. I guess I wasn't good luck for them." I look for similarity in her face now, softer with age, lined with smiles and anger.

My face, too, has changed with the years. I see my seven year old niece in my pictures—sweet, open-eyed. My teenage pictures radiate with innocent happiness. I notice the difference in my older smile. "I am sitting here wanting memories to teach me," sing Sweet Honey and the Rock.

I have shared a photo album of Integrity Moments with you, telling you the stories behind the pictures. Maybe you better understand the slightly pinched smile, the sad profile, the joyous abandon you see. Maybe you remember your own stories, which I hope you will share with me.

These snapshots of stories reveal our Integrity Moments. Some of the stories represent moments when we acted with less integrity, others are ripe with it. The stories signal key choice points in our life, when something about who we were at that time was at stake. Other stories are full of everyday moments, revealing our joys and mistakes in learning to be ourselves.

We study pictures from a photo album to learn who we are— what our identity is—and to remember how the world looked during that moment in time—our perception. The collection of photos represents our Personal Tradition of Integrity, how the Integrity Moments of our lives accumulate to make you you and me me.

Because each photo represents moments which were often important, we may not stop reflecting on them when the situation concludes. Often the memory of the moment can last for days and even years. As growing, self-correcting systems, we strive to learn from our experiences.

What's worked in the past? What hasn't? What do we learn about our integrity when we act consistently with core values and principles and when we don't? As you browse through the photos of your past, what have you learned?

How can we convert a less than satisfying experience, so we won't repeat the consequences? Are we experiencing a loop or cycle of Integrity Moments, borrowing from its predecessors? How does this moment build on or shift our Personal Tradition of Integrity?

Learning takes many forms. We learn from the consequences of our behavior, advise and mentor others based on our learning, shift our perceptions due to a learning moment, and work to convert a current negative experience for a more satisfying resolution of future Integrity Moments.

LEARNING FROM CONSEQUENCES

We learn from the consequences of our decisions and actions during an Integrity Moment. These consequences may be positive or not, may have moved us forward or not. Understanding something new about ourselves and our identity can influence our future choices and action.

SETTING INTENTIONS

When Kelly suspected her colleagues of taking kick-backs in an early work experience, she learned about who she was and what was important to her. "I came away with a better understanding that there is a difference between perception and reality.

"You can't always escape what a perceived reality is at the time. But I do think you have to cling to your reality and your value system so you can stay tuned to who you are. You need to know what your bottom line is, so that even if you decide to proceed beyond that, you know that you have made that choice."

Developing an intention to stay in touch with her values and know when she has crossed her bottom line into a personally unacceptable area has influenced her subsequent Integrity Moments. She relies on previous experiences as a "blueprint" to guide her choices, building her Personal Tradition of Integrity.

USING FEEDBACK AND SELF-REFLECTION TO CHANGE

The learning process may involve self-reflection or feedback from another person. A potential girlfriend told Max "that she really would have preferred being with me, but my temper was too bad. I thought, 'well, that's good information.' My temper was bad because I was in pain all of the time from fear of abuse by my father and aunt who were very temperamental. Kids tend to imitate what they see around them.

"If my temper was altering my life now, I decided it was only going to get worse. I decided to work on altering that and start getting in tune with changing my responses, and consequently my behavior. It was good that I did, because this happened when I was about fifteen. I was in the Army by the time I was seventeen. If I hadn't started to self-regulate, I would've been so out of control that I would've ended up in Army prison."

While in the Army, Max also refined his distinction between healthy anger and abusive anger. He recognized he was being mistreated by an officer. "I decided, hey, I'm not going to get pushed around. I'm going to learn different coping skills and strategies to deal with people so I don't have to put up with this. I might get the same abuse, but how I respond to them, and what I do about it is going to be different from here on in."

Max uses both feedback and self-reflection to learn from the consequences of his actions and then sets an intention to grow and change. With intentional practice, he can shift his own and others' perceptions as well.

STRATEGY TIME

Try this experiment. Next time you find yourself in one of those familiar situations, whatever it may be, be aware. "A-ha! Here's a time when I tend to react out of habit." Slow down. Think about the outcome you want. How is that similar or different from what you usually get as an end result? Set your intention based on your desired outcome.

Now, lay out your options. Develop a set of at least three. One choice means you're stuck—that's the old behavior. Two choices creates a dilemma—either this or that. With three options, you start to have choice. Which option helps you best enact your intention? Go for it, and learn from what happens.

LEARNING BY SHIFTING PERCEPTIONS

Shifting from Small to Big centers on changing your perception of who you are in relationship to the situation you are facing. In Chapter 3, I shared several strategies for shifting your perceptions. Going through the conscious exercise of changing how you experience a situation can provide major learning that influences future Integrity Moments.

Patricia Williams recalls a childhood experience of literally shifting how and what she saw:

> One summer when I was about six, my family drove to Maine. The highway was straight and hot and shimmered darkly in the sun. My sister and I sat in the back seat of the Studebaker and argued about what color the road was. I said black, she said purple. I was unimpressed with the relevance of that at the time; but with the passage of years, and much more observation, I have come to see endless over-heated highways as slightly more purple than black. My sister and I will probably argue about the hue of life's roads forever. But the lesson I learned from listening to her wild perceptions is that it really is possible to see things—even the most concrete things—simultaneously yet differently; and that seeing simultaneously yet differently is more easily done by two people than one, but that one person can get the hang of it with time and effort.

With the strategies presented in this book as well as your own, changing perceptions of yourself and your life's road is doable with awareness and intention.

From the personal photos shared in Chapter 3, let me demonstrate how the reframe might happen. Several of my Small stories center on losing my voice, not speaking up for myself and dealing poorly with perceived authority.

Look at the photos again. Start with my experience in high school as a co-editor. Continue in college with my boyfriend who told me off. Then during graduate school, Ken asked me to collaborate in an experiment that involved me being quiet, followed by the Gethsemani experience and Joanne.

The theme these photos reveal is withdrawing into silence. Not one I'm proud of. Now I see the experiences quite differently. I notice that through these Small stories, I have actually come to my voice. I now know how to use it. Without these experiences, I might not have learned how.

With my high school co-editor, I haven't received any closure. Studiously avoiding high school reunions, whether she's there or not, has been my continual choice. While a distant memory, a yellowing photo in my photo album, it lingers unresolved.

During the first six months after college, then at the time of our 10 year reunion, and most recently just two years ago, I reached out to my college boyfriend, although he chose not to respond each time. This past attempt, I wrote him a note apologizing for whatever I had done to spark such anger and resentment and let him know I forgave him for hurting me at the time. Although I haven't heard from him, I nevertheless feel closure about that painful period.

With Ken, I needed two years to reconcile with him about my self-destruction in our graduate program. But I'm proud that I didn't leave the program with that painful thread loose so that it might trip me in the future.

And with Joanne, I reduced the period before I spoke out about all my complex feelings to just a few hours. That is progress! From this perspective, I haven't lost my voice, but actually am gaining it.

What's next? Why, being able to speak out in the moment itself. And I'm getting much better at that. As I practice based on the awareness of all the earlier photos in my photo album, my intention to use my voice to stand up for who I am and my integrity is strong.

By shifting my attitude, my point of view, my perspective, I also shift my perception from Small to Big. By asking what have I learned here, I expand my view of the world and my place in it.

As a result, I reframe how I see those photos from victim to opportunity, including developing my ability to use my voice proactively and positively in potentially confrontive situations.

With the renewed awareness that I do author my own experiences, I give myself permission to re-organize my world and my encounters with it differently. Focusing attention on what I can learn helps me choose to better tolerate the less-than-delightful embedded in these kinds of situations.

Does this mean that once the lesson has been learned, I will never withdraw and lose my voice again? Probably not. But my guess is I will be able to shift perceptions and make more integrity-enhancing choices more quickly.

STRATEGY TIME

If you find yourself in a victim situation, the butt of a bad deal, take a moment to reframe. How else can you view who you are in this situation? What's funny about what's happening? What is there to learn here?

How would Superman view the situation? What would Katherine Hepburn do? How about Mother Theresa? Notice how trying on different points of view changes your experience.

LEARNING CONVERTS TO ADVISING AND MENTORING

In addition to learning something about yourself from the consequences of your experiences and by shifting perceptions, you may want to pass your learning on to others. By sharing your own stories, you can demonstrate how others can have positive experiences. In other words, you become a mentor and advisor.

Once Kelly was encouraged by a supervisor to push forward and to pursue her doctoral education. "Kelly's supervisor said, 'here's a piece of advice to think about. Don't close any doors on yourself. Too many other people are willing to do that. You have to be willing to walk through those doors. Even if others close them, you have to be willing to break them open to go through. But don't be your own worst enemy.'

"I really thought about it. Particularly as a woman, I realized that many people of both sexes were willing to close doors on me. I kept debating it. But her words kept coming back. Was I closing doors on myself? How important was it for me to be flexible? How important was it to take risks and options that were presented?"

Now, as a popular lecturer, Kelly teaches others this basic powerful message. "I've been able to share that with other young women who are making decisions about their own career paths and personal lives. Sometimes they are the only ones holding themselves back. You have to overcome society's roadblocks. Why should you help put those barriers up?"

Shirley also wants to prevent others from encountering the hardships she faced. This Jewish grandmother felt compromised during her own wedding more than fifty years ago. She and her fiance wanted a quiet Justice of the Peace wedding, yet her future father-in-law insisted on a traditional wedding with a Rabbi.

When her own daughter announced her upcoming marriage, she decided "that I better not let my feelings about anything influence her. Then I said to her, 'what do you want?' She said, 'we don't want anything. We are going to go to court.' Then some friends said that they really would like to throw a party. So they made a potluck. It was fairly low key. My daughter was also making compromises. But whatever she wanted was fine with me."

She reflected on her own stressful wedding day and rather than risk creating that same unhappiness, she supported her daughter's choices. Instead of perpetuating a Small experience, she created a new, more satisfying Big moment.

STRATEGY TIME

Be aware of opportunities when you can share learning from your own experience to benefit others. Notice also when you can back off, let go, and support others in making their own decisions. Both demonstrate the generosity of spirit of being Big.

LEARNING CONVERTS TO BEING BIG

Often after acting inconsistently with our basic principles and values, we learn from the experience by contemplating how we might have acted differently. Recognizing the situation as a learning opportunity, we work to convert some aspect of the experience to align more closely with what's important to us.

In other words, we strive to make the inconsistent experience more consistent. Employing the strategies from this chapter—learning from consequences, learning through shifted perceptions, and using learning to mentor and advise others—we reinterpret our experiences or choose follow-up actions that shift our Integrity Moment toward Big-ness.

Our learning results in new awarenesses, followed by an intention to act differently the next time. We may also renew our commitment to or clarify our most important values and principles through concrete experience.

WITH REFLECTION

After reflecting on the situation and her values, Vicki, a health care administrator, shifted her perceptions. She reacted strongly when a long phone conversation with a patient ended when he got obscene. "I guess I just learned that people are different, and you're going to run into that kind of thing.

"I just can't take it personally because even though what he said was so very personal, it wasn't about me. I don't think he really meant it at me. He never met me. I was just a voice."

Although Vicki panicked in the moment, which left her feeling Small, she learned to ask, "is this about me?" Next time, she expects to react more calmly and consistently with her values.

DISCOVERING VALUES HIERARCHIES

Sandra learned something important about herself and how to prioritize her values in the Small experience with her second husband. "He hasn't been as warm or kind to my children as I had hoped he would be. He was going to see his daughter, and he wanted me to go with him. I'd told him all along I wasn't going to go, because I felt, and this isn't like me to say, because you don't do this, I'm not going to do that. But I didn't act the way I normally would.

"I said, 'when you can start treating my daughter and the boys the way I have always treated your daughters, then I will think about going with you again.' Well maybe it was a turning point for me. I was able to stick to my decision, as much as I don't act that way. It made me realize that I can't give up my kids and my family just because he's rude."

Sandra's learning to stand up for a value she holds dear—regard for her children. She's experimenting with taking a stand in other aspects of this relationship, too. Learning from this inconsistent experience and establishing firm, clear boundaries have been pivotal for helping shape how Sandra resolves future dilemmas.

SETTING BOUNDARIES

In saying "no" to working the day before a holiday, Mona, a hair stylist, felt like she violated her own work ethic. Yet "I'm glad I said 'no'. I felt good taking care of myself, which is so different from how I usually act. I still have a tendency to be a people pleaser, and then forget about me.

"It felt okay, it is okay. My boss will get over it. If he doesn't, that is his stuff not mine." In reflecting on her Small experience, Mona learned the benefit of saying 'no' to support another of her important values, self-care.

FOLLOW-UP ACTION

Samuel, a young manager on the manufacturing shop floor, has been challenged by his seasoned long-term employees and disparities between his standards of work and theirs. After a loud argument with one of those employees, he worked to shift a Small situation.

"Me being young, I haven't seen everything. Sometimes I lack good communication skills, and walls get thrown up in certain areas. It has hurt me." But Sam has been committed to being a great manager, and so he took action.

"I'd like to settle the differences, make things right and explain my situation. Let him explain his situation to me, so I can be a little more understanding. And that's what happened. I explained to him why I got upset, and I apologized for being unprofessional. It actually made us a little closer."

By having this awkward conversation, Sam begins forging stronger working relationships. Each time he practices, the same kind of conversation will get easier. He also has developed a renewed commitment to his values and these strategies for working with difficult employees, all as a result of his inconsistent experience.

STRATEGY TIME

What unfinished business can you clean up? Pick one instance—perhaps with a colleague or neighbor, child or a friend.

Start by reviewing the circumstance from this perspective of the present. The situation is in the past. What do you know now that you didn't know then? How do those insights effect your thoughts and feelings about the situation? What resources are you aware of now, both internal and external, that weren't present at the time?

Based on this renewed perspective, what can you say to the other person? Take ownership of your part of the situation. Be honest and apologize for whatever you are truly sorry for. Lead with your integrity and expect the other person to meet you there. Experience how the relationship shifts and how your own internal sense of completion creates new energy. Congratulations!

LEARNING AND OPTIMISM

Learners are optimists at work, actively applying non-negative thinking to become Big again. Non-negative thinking allows you to move from being Small to recovering your Big-ness. Your state of mind is one clue for gaining and maintaining size control. I think this is what Alice in Wonderland learned about nibbling the correct side of the mushroom.

Of the storytellers, only two of the women who criticized themselves in the Small moments described their inconsistent experiences as learning opportunities. I'm reminded of Martin Seligman's theory on learned optimism. Through laboratory research, he demonstrated how both optimism and helplessness are almost always learned reactions.

Learned helplessness equates to a quitting response, a giving up reaction. Pessimism perpetuates learned helplessness when we personalize disappointing results, blame ourselves, and label negative outcomes as permanent. These qualities are similar to the self-critical pattern.

Optimists, on the other hand, learn to ignore or work with those harsh internal voices. Learned optimism works through the power of non-negative thinking, demonstrated, for example, by learning from Small experiences.

Looking through one more photo album, maybe Norma Desmond from *Sunset Boulevard* says it best. The silent film star who faded with talkies meets a journalist. William Holden playing Joe Gillis says, "I know you. You're Norma Desmond. You used to be big."

Gloria Swanson as Norma replies, "I am big. It's the pictures that have gotten small."

STRATEGY TIME

If you find yourself using the word 'always,' catch yourself. Nothing is 'always' true. Try saying, "in the past, this was 'always' true." Notice how your language frees up your choicefulness in the present.

Play with the language of the optimist. Instead of "this is impossible for me," try "this *has been* impossible for me." Experience the difference.

"I just can't get started in the morning." Think of all the times you've had absolutely no trouble getting started in the morning. Data disputes the 'can't' in the statement. How liberating. 'Can' and 'can't' are about capability and competence. You are perfectly capable of getting started in the morning.

By paying attention to our language, we learn what limits us and shapes our sense of pessimism. We learn how to break free to create possibility in the present so we can defy past experience. Even if you feel silly, repeat your statement out loud with the revised language. Train your mind to think differently, and your actions will follow.

Learning in The Integrity Moment

Learning occurs . . .

- through consequences
- by shifting perceptions
- for advising and mentoring
- by converting to being Big

Coming up in Chapter 8, we look at how learning collects into your Personal Tradition of Integrity. First, play with the Personal Applications that follow to explore your own learning patterns.

FURTHER READING AND VIEWING

Seligman, M.E.P. (1991). *Learned Optimism*. New York: Alfred A. Knopf.

Sunset Boulevard (1950). Paramount Pictures.

Williams, P.J. (1991). *The Alchemy of Race and Rights*. Cambridge: Harvard University Press.

PERSONAL APPLICATION

Create your own photo album of Integrity Moments in your mind's eye. Refer to your timeline from p. 87 if helpful. Now flip through the pages of your photo album, reflecting on what you have learned about yourself and how to interact with others.

How have you applied your learning?

Now reflect on a current Integrity Moment that has captured your attention. What other similar moments have you faced in the past?

What were the outcomes then? What happened?

How can you apply what you learned then to this current situation?

PERSONAL APPLICATION

Reflect on a current issue in your life. This issue may involve some aspect of your career, your personal life, a financial situation, your spiritual life, health, physical environment, personal development, your family or any other aspect of your life. Give the issue a brief name, to fill in the blank below. Use the factors effecting the Integrity Moment to gain new insights.

_____ Moment

	Not at All Important		Somewhat Important		Very Important
Take a stand	1	2	3	4	5
Speak out	1	2	3	4	5
Clear boundaries	1	2	3	4	5
Desire to influence	1	2	3	4	5
Feel overwhelmed	1	2	3	4	5
Lack choice	1	2	3	4	5
Avoid contact	1	2	3	4	5
Suppress your voice	1	2	3	4	5
Effortful behavior	1	2	3	4	5
Automatic behavior	1	2	3	4	5
Generosity of spirit	1	2	3	4	5
Negative self-criticism	1	2	3	4	5

What can you learn from and for this moment?

PERSONAL APPLICATION

Reflect on a key relationship in your life. This relationship might be with a partner, boss, spouse, physician, mechanic, co-worker, child, neighbor, friend, etc. Assess who you are in this relationship.

Relationship: _____

	Not at All Present		Somewhat Present		Very Present
Take a stand	1	2	3	4	5
Speak out	1	2	3	4	5
Clear boundaries	1	2	3	4	5
Desire to influence	1	2	3	4	5
Feel overwhelmed	1	2	3	4	5
Lack choice	1	2	3	4	5
Avoid contact	1	2	3	4	5
Suppress your voice	1	2	3	4	5
Effortful behavior	1	2	3	4	5
Automatic behavior	1	2	3	4	5
Generosity of spirit	1	2	3	4	5
Negative self-critique	1	2	3	4	5

What can you learn from and for this relationship?

THE PERSONAL
TRADITION OF INTEGRITY

I sit in the power of our stories. I sit in wonder for their beauty, sweetness, strength and good-heartedness. The stories are ripe and juicy with wisdom. I've wandered through the stories to make meaning from others' and my own experiences for what we can learn about our Integrity Moments.

The Integrity Moment centers on your identity and perception. Who are you, and what is important to you, now, in this moment? How do you perceive yourself in relationship to the situation you face?

You have explored a variety of themes that comprise the Integrity Moment. Looking across your life at the choice points that involved your basic values and principles, you've learned something about the nature of your identity and how it shapes and is shaped by your integrity.

Resolving your Integrity Moments in a satisfying way often involves listening to and following your Authentic Self—"this is who I am and how I want to be." You may know who you are in opposition to some person, thing or event. "I absolutely am not that, so I must be this."

Who is involved can also influence how you resolve your Integrity Moments. At times, you are open to allowing a pivotal person to enter your story and influence its outcome. At other times, even in similar circumstances, you strongly want to proceed on your own without counsel and be self-reliant.

As you delve into the sweet complexity of your own Integrity Moments, you notice that how you perceive yourself helps determine whether or not you have integrity in the moment. Acting consistently with your basic values and principles, you are Big in your situation. You can take an active stance, marked by effortful behavior, creating a space for generosity of spirit toward yourself and others.

When you are Small and your situation looms large, you can fall into disempowerment, behave automatically rather than effortfully and shrink into a space too small to include such generosity. In fact, you may be predisposed to negatively criticize yourself. When Small, you are more inclined to act inconsistently with your basic values and principles.

The Integrity Moment is . . .		
an identity-making process	and	a perceptual process
Who am I in this moment?		*I am Big*
		ME > situation
		I am Small
		me < SITUATION

The process of working with all the stories has guided me into these fresh insights about integrity. As murky shadows lift from your reflecting pool of integrity, you can see not only a particular Integrity Moment reflected back more clearly, but also your Personal Tradition of Integrity, in the clearing lagoon of your experience. Sunlight sparkling on your Personal Tradition of Integrity is like the sun's rays shining on a slowly growing crystal, creating momentary prisms.

A SLOWLY GROWING CRYSTAL OF EXPERIENCE

I study the clear quartz crystal dangling in front of my office's large picture window. Throughout the year, it throws rainbows around the room with the passage of the sun, each sunny day's prism slightly different than the previous.

Contemplating the crystal, I think of the complexity of who I am in my world as a subtle shift from Integrity Moment to Integrity

Moment. I learn from the crystal—how the light hits it determines the nature, strength and placement of its prism.

So, too, is the outcome of my Integrity Moment dependent upon how light shines upon it. The stories may point to themes that look like either-or dualities. Either I am Big or I am Small. Either I behave effortfully or automatically. Either I am open to a pivotal person or I am self-contained.

Actually, each of these features or qualities of the Integrity Moment form a point on a three-dimensional quartz crystal. Which ones are involved in forming a reflected prism of color depends on how the light shines on the crystal.

Imagine the possible combinations of crystallized points forming an Integrity Moment. Perhaps a pivotal person enters, I know something about myself in opposition to that person, and I find new ways to behave effortfully. Maybe I am striking out for the independence of being self-reliant, take an active stance, and feel overwhelmed. Or I gain a new insight about myself as I become aware of my habitual, reactive behaviors.

Creating rigid, fixed and polarized opposites over-simplifies our experiences in the Integrity Moment. Instead, a crystal lives, grows and changes into a myriad of shapes. How we perceive it depends on where we stand in relation to it.

Like the King of Siam, from *The King and I*, who no longer knows what he knows, I have passed through many stages of not-knowing during this Integrity Moment inquiry. The subtlety of the crystal helps me avoid the risk of over-generalizing from a set number of stories by capturing the paradox of a simultaneous crystallized light of clarity and not-knowing.

The light of your situation shines on your personal crystal, highlighting certain experiences, perspectives, and qualities of mind, heart and spirit. You hold the crystal, which captures your Integrity Moments and your particular interpretations, as it slowly grows to form your Personal Tradition of Integrity.

THE INTEGRITY CYCLE

Your Personal Tradition of Integrity builds and grows throughout your life. Your Integrity Moments and the meaning you make of them are inherent to this building and growth process. Each experience of integrity—each Integrity Moment—makes the next similar moment you face a bit more familiar, with a relevant history of learning for you to draw upon.

In this way, integrity has a self-reinforcing quality, deepening your sense of yourself as you cycle from experience to experience, from Integrity Moment to Integrity Moment. The integrity cycle is directly linked to your identity and your perception of who you are in the world.

Once in the cycle of integrity, you will notice how much easier the dilemmas of Integrity Moments are resolved and how quickly you learn from them. Acting with integrity, when you are in an integrity cycle, flows more naturally. Like building a muscle, awareness and practice strengthens the cycle.

This reinforcing cycle forms the tradition of your integrity—your personal history of Integrity Moments that you draw upon in the present and future. Your Personal Tradition of Integrity develops throughout your life, becoming richer and more resonant with the result of each experience, whether that experience has or lacks integrity.

Is the light that shines on your crystal of integrity totally beyond your control? What role can you actively play in developing your Personal Tradition of Integrity? How can you be Big more often in life?

Answers to these questions rely on your effortful process of making powerful interpretations about yourself in the situation. This personal power comes by heightening self-awareness, determining your intentions, remembering the power of choice, having the courage to commit and act upon a choice, and effortfully engaging in learning from your experiences. These qualities describe the integrity cycle—the moving, growing, changing part of your Personal Tradition of Integrity.

HEIGHTENING AWARENESS OF YOUR INTEGRITY MOMENTS

A first step for you to make the powerful interpretation during an Integrity Moment involves recognizing that this moment is important. Just reading and working through this book zooms up your awareness of daily Integrity Moments. You may that realize something important about you is at stake nearly all the time. This awareness opens up new possibilities, as explored below.

Integrity involves operating out of your truth, becoming more fully who you are—a most important life task. But how do you know what specifically makes up your inner truth, and how do you live with the difficulties that may impede your ability to act with integrity? Some answers come from self-reflection and self-acceptance.

SELF-REFLECTION

In my frenzied life, slowing down long enough to listen inside represents a major challenge. Is this true for you, too? Naturally, we experience our culture's bias toward action as opposed to reflection.

As much as I want to live an inside-out life, with my behavior motivated by my deeply held values and principles, I'm too often distracted by the pressures, deadlines and realities of situations I create while following my values-centered dreams. In this ironic struggle, I am reminded of the haiku I wrote when introducing myself at the beginning of a workshop:

> Distant rain, wind-burn,
> Climbing ladders to see beyond.
> Learn to love plateaus.

Learning to love my plateaus, just where I am now, is recognition of my need for self-reflection in the ongoing search for awareness in the moment. Trying to live as an 'on-purpose' person, anchored to my core values and beliefs, sometimes makes ladder climbing seem a lot easier.

123

In addition, I find that I am absolutely brilliant at reflecting on my Integrity Moments after the fact, no matter how wildly I flounder during the moment itself. Allowing self-reflection to influence me in the moment is certainly part of my conscious learning and growth process.

Loving plateaus involves consciousness and mindfulness in 'the here and now.' Those of us, like me, who are goal-oriented, future and dream motivated, can be challenged and even resistant to such present-oriented thinking. Yet I believe that recognizing and living through those resistances is key to more responsiveness in the moment, so that more of our Integrity Moments resolve successfully.

RESISTANCE AND ACCEPTANCE

You may resist self-reflection. You may be concerned about losing control or dealing with uncertainty, confusion, loss of face, a sense of incompetence, past resentments and other fears. How much easier to just act habitually in the situation rather than stay present to its complexities, even though our automatic behavior can leave us feeling Small.

In Gestalt therapy practice, as taught by the Gestalt Institute of Cleveland, resistances are honored as part of our ongoing functioning. Once raised to your awareness, you can then question whether the resistance is helpful and even desirable. With awareness, your potential for choosing a different behavior is greatly increased. Even if you choose the resistance, you are making a choice, rather than acting from habit.

An interim step emerges prior to making a different choice: you will be hard pressed to make a change, until you thoroughly accept who, what and how you are. I don't want to minimize how difficult self-acceptance is. Again with a culture that creates expectations of Super Mom and Dapper Dad, we may find ourselves constantly seeking change in our bodies, in our relationships, in our performance, in our lives.

Small moments further promote a strong tendency to be self-critical. Messages of "I am not good enough, smart enough, perfect enough" can readily mingle in our experiences. Non-negative thinking, introduced in Chapter 7, is one component for allowing self-acceptance.

Letting go of resistance and self-criticism not only may be difficult, but also uncomfortable, typical of changes to the familiar. I believe that successfully resolving your Integrity Moments depends upon your self-acceptance that you are doing the best you can in this moment. With self-reflection and acceptance of what you learn as a result, you open the door for more flexibility and responsiveness in the moment, creating choices that help align your actions with your basic values and principles.

Three years ago, I learned a life lesson about self-acceptance. While I was facing a work deadline, my grandfather passed away, one month shy of his 97th birthday. We were all aware he was failing, so for the previous several months, I tried to cultivate landmarks, like visits home, for him to look forward to.

When my father called late one night, even before answering the phone, I knew what had happened. At that time, I was struggling with major life transitions and time pressures. I was crazed. Yet, instantly I knew what to do.

Regardless of what deadlines I would miss and what financial impact that might result in, I was headed to Dallas to be with my family. In that moment, my priorities re-aligned, and my stress disappeared. My grandfather took it with him.

That family visit was simultaneously one of the most emotionally difficult yet satisfying of many a year. I felt Big on that trip. Upon my return, re-facing my life's pandemonium, I deeply accepted my choices, my priorities and my tradeoffs. Grandpa's gift—a renewed spiritual self-acceptance.

STRATEGY TIME

Being more responsive to yourself and what is important to you during the Integrity Moment comes from a foundation of awareness through self-reflection and self-acceptance. First, recognize when you are in a Small moment, either during or as soon after the moment as possible. Acknowledge your Big-ness or Small-ness. Notice the differences you experience when you are

Small versus when you are Big. Don't try to change your responses yet. Simply be aware.

For me, inner-responsiveness to avoid having inconsistent moments means paying attention to my intuitive and physical warning signals that something is amiss here. Is my inner voice screaming, "no, no!"? Am I holding my breath or clenching my stomach?

I'm learning that these are sure signs that I'm heading into the disempowerment of a Small experience. What are your signals? How you respond to make the powerful interpretation and choice while still in the moment is explored below.

But first, learn your personal cues and signs that you are facing an Integrity Moment. For a week, try keeping a log of your Integrity Moments and note the clues and signals that indicated you were entering, experiencing or resolving one.

Get to know the various parts of yourself. Is there a part of you that negatively critiques your performance? What is the positive intention of this part? How does this part want you to be? This part is only one of your internal Board of Directors. What other parts can advise you during this Integrity Moment?

SETTING YOUR INTENTION

Healers believe that crystals have magical properties, including a consciousness which absorbs and acts on intentions. I believe the same for the crystal of your integrity. Staying close to your intentions gives you the basis for acting consistently with your values and principles.

Intention starts with awareness. With awareness of the integrity strategies that work and don't work, you can more clearly determine what you want in terms of the process and outcome of your Integrity Moments. In other words, your intention centers on discerning what you want.

In any particular moment, you are doing the best you can. You certainly don't consciously think, "ah, now I'm going to figure out how to be unhappy." Instead you are living life as well as you know how, with intention to create a good life for yourself, however you define that.

Despite fears and insecurities which might lead us to be hurtful to ourselves and others, I believe people are intrinsically good and move in a basically positive direction. Whenever I get hooked by someone else's behavior, I remind myself to separate the person from the behavior and then ask, what is this person's intention? Most often, it is not to hurt me.

Set your intention to have more integrity in your life. From a spiritual perspective, manifesting your dreams, goals and desires come from setting just such clear intentions. Your intentions may also be further clarified and refined by the choices you discover in the situation. Clear intentions mark the path for integrity.

STRATEGY TIME

To manifest what you want in your life, first reflect on what makes a good life for you. What is the first step for having what you want? What qualities, values and principles do you want more of in your life? Remember that your 'wants' may be very different from your 'should's'.

Now take a moment and prioritize your top wants. Select three. Affirmations are one way to set and manifest your intentions. Write three affirmations, one for each of your top three wants. Affirmations are "I" statements that are stated in the positive and the present tense. They are concrete and specific whenever possible.

For example, my daily affirmations have included a specific statement of how much income I want each month, worded as "I am a successful Life Coach making at least $x per month." As an example of a different kind of affirmation, I also say, "I have an open mind."

Say your affirmations out loud three times daily. Repetition as well as hearing yourself say the statements are both powerful.

You may even want to look at yourself in the mirror as you say them to visually reinforce your want. You can have what you want.

REMEMBER THE POWER OF CHOICE

Making the Big interpretation of a situation may involve reframing your action as a choice, not as an inevitability, and using your peripheral vision to open up your options. Both approaches support converting your heightened self-awareness and clear intention into greater inner-responsiveness in the moment.

REFRAMING AS A CHOICE

I make myself Small when I lose sight of my choices in a situation. When I perceive a lack of choices, I start to get a little sick—physically, emotionally, mentally, spiritually. On the far side of those moments, I often realize that I always had choices and was not resourceful enough in the moment to find them.

The same may be true for you. Often our inconsistent moments center on a perceived lack of choice, and like me, you may not be particularly proud of those moments. Opportunity lies in reframing, that is, shifting our perceptions to make our available choices more apparent.

Varying attitudes about how much you can control your destiny may affect your sense of choicefulness. Some say that fate determines the outcome of situations, while others believe that you can be and are responsible for results. These attitudes vary by culture. Which style best fits your beliefs?

Based on his experience in a Nazi concentration camp, Viktor Frankl teaches that no matter how dire your circumstances, you always have the choice to shift your perspective. At a minimum, at all times, you have control over your attitude and how you experience and interpret your situation. He demonstrated how the power of choice gave him strength to survive trauma and actually saved his life.

Even on a less egregious level, you can remember that being a victim in a situation is actually a choice you make. Stuckness, or perceived lack of choice, can actually be an easy choice because it allows you to abdicate responsibility and be a victim. Thinking that outcomes of your experiences are beyond your control is a form of learned helplessness, one possible cause of clinical depression.

So when you seem stuck, what other choices can you make? What is the Big choice?

I learned the hard way—through painful moments which lacked integrity—that I always have the power to reframe and create choice. I certainly went through the helpless victim stage before leaving my first career and my first doctoral program. I'm aware of how completely I created my own raw experiences.

No one but me chose to be a victim or a cynic, eliminating my own power in the process of making myself Small. What were my choices early on during these Integrity Moments? Caught in a kind of blindness about my options, I continued to operate in that perceived choiceless mode until the only choice I left myself in both cases was to leave the system. Truly, what a waste of energy, yet also a source of tremendous personal learning.

To participate fully in your life, recognize and broaden your choices in any given circumstance. Take responsibility for yourself and your choices, for authoring your life and for giving meaning to your Integrity Moments. Develop a facility and flexibility for reframing how you view yourself and your situation.

Positive self-esteem, that internal mechanism for judging yourself positively, boosts choices as well. When negatively self-critical, this internal critic may tell you that you have no choice at all, and you may temporarily lose your ability to reframe the situation. In contrast, creating and acting on choices feed positive self-assessments, which in turn make creating choices easier.

Try non-negative thinking to hike esteem. For example, my friend Alice, who's been attending Hebrew classes for years, recently mentioned that she was thinking about stopping since she never did the homework and wasn't progressing as quickly as she would like. Because she deeply values productivity, her inner critic was loudly berating her.

But Alice really enjoys the class, the other participants and being part of a learning environment. Once she reframed her reasons for taking the class to these qualities, her inner critic quieted down, and she revamped her enjoyment.

Rather than sacrifice her pleasure, Alice now feels better about her choices as well as with herself. Actively working and playing to reframe situations and widening your peripheral vision are ways to break the negative cycle of low self-esteem and perceived lack of choice.

Using Peripheral Vision

Seeing possibilities is part of creating choice. As with your actual eyesight, while in a stuck place, you may not be using your peripheral vision. Working with stuckness hinges on shifting how you see, how wide your lens is, so that you can see with 'new eyes.' Awareness of how you perceive is the basis for constructing yourself and the world.

I like Hugh Huntington's peripheral vision story of the Aztec wide angle lens. The Aztecs were successful at invading forts because they entered holding themselves in unexpected, and even strange, body positions. The fort guards were trained to look for certain forms of invasion, such as stealthy creeping, and consequently, were unable to see the more flamboyant entries by the Aztecs.

So, too, are you unable to see the unusual, the possible, if you are only looking for certain, expected options. When Huntington tells about the Aztecs, he demonstrates how to use our peripheral vision. Would you like to try?

Frame your eyes with your hands, angled forward, like blinders on a horse. Now, very slowly open your hands to the side, while keeping your focus fixed straight ahead. What do you notice now as you continue to look straight ahead? Can you see more of the room than you did before this exercise?

This process of opening allows you to see with your peripheral vision, as well as take in the object of your focus. You literally learn to broaden your seeing, to see more, to see differently—to see your additional choices.

Your choices help form the crystal of your Personal Tradition of Integrity. Your ability to see choices says something about who you are in this moment, as well as what is important to you. Every choice involves saying 'yes' to some thing and 'no' to something else and so represents a fork in your path. Your choices are actually, in reality, choosing the kind of person you are becoming.

Heightening your awareness in the moment, setting your intention, and choosing to have choice provide a base for how you hold the crystal of your integrity tradition. How you hold the crystal affects how the light shines through it, creating the prism of your experience during the Integrity Moment.

STRATEGY TIME

Feeling stuck? Take a few moments to make a metaphoric cherry pie and cut it into eight slices. What are eight different choices you have in this moment? Make sure to include one choice as 'stay stuck.' Feel free to include outrageous options like 'fail' and 'move to Sydney, Australia.' Often the unusual can spring open your creative door to finding new options.

Watch your language. One way to limit your choices is to use the words 'but' and 'or.' Both words set up restrictions, stops and jolts. 'But' negates the first part of your sentence: "I would love to help you, but my boss wouldn't like it." 'Or' sets up only two possibilities: "Either I can help you, or I can keep my job."

Experience what happens when you substitute the word 'and' for your 'but's and 'or's.' For example, "I would love to help you, and my boss won't like it. What do we do now?" Notice if you open up more possibilities and choices.

BRING COURAGE TO ACTION

Staying close to your intentions and creating an array of choices give you courage to act consistently with your values and principles. Intention feeds courage. While selecting one choice may involve a back-and-forth dance with your intention—which choice best fits my intention, and how do my choices affect my intention?—clarity of each provides you with the resolve to move forward.

Your intentionality makes courage and then effective action possible, diffusing paralyzing helplessness. Through courage, your intentions manifest into action, which gradually builds your Personal Tradition of Integrity.

Courage to act takes many forms—courage to be yourself, for self-awareness and self-reflection, to admit when you don't understand, to accept responsibility for your own behavior and the consequences of your behavior, to change your behavior, to act on your own behalf, and to persist even when the going gets tough.

Look at all the stories in this book that have involved courage—taking a stand in the face of opposition, speaking out, establishing clear boundaries and striving to influence others. Courage helps you trust your intuition. Allowing someone to openly influence your life takes courage, as does self-reliance. Imagine the courage necessary to share moments of pain, to self-disclose weakness.

A major moment of courage for me was moving out of choice-lessness into owning my experience during my graduate program. To eliminate blame directed at others required taking responsibility for the role I played in creating my own difficult experience. When have you felt oppressed by your situation? Who is the oppressor, and how responsible are you for your own liberation?

Courage gave me the freedom to risk moving beyond my self-imposed limitations. I hope the same for you.

Having the courage to self-reflect and accept yourself creates your inner-responsiveness in the moment and shapes the slowly growing crystal of your Personal Tradition of Integrity. Being a courageous warrior is not about being aggressive, but rather is about being Big in your world, being choiceful, and having the fierce courage to commit to and act on those choices and learn from the consequences.

STRATEGY TIME

Acting with courage involves commitment to your intention and your desired choice. Commitment can be easier if you enlist the support of others, either formally with a coach or counselor or informally. Tell a friend, partner or co-worker what you are going to do. Ask them to follow up with you in a week or so, to check-in on your courage.

Write your commitments down. Say them out loud each day, like affirmations. In your home or office, stand in a doorway facing a room. Imagine that behind you is fear, pain, cowardice or any other challenge to your courage. The room in front of you is the room of courage.

With great intention, read your commitments out loud and step into the room. Take the commitment plunge. After declaring your commitments, celebrate who you are becoming with your courageous actions.

THE LEARNING FOR INTEGRITY CYCLES

Making the powerful interpretation of your Integrity Moment provides you with an opportunity to learn from the consequences, however challenging, of your actions. As a learning being, you can delve into the meaning of your principles and values in relationship to your current experience with self-awareness and courage, knowing that you are shaping your future behavior.

One Buddhist saying offers that "pain is inevitable, suffering is optional." Powerful learning comes from the interpretations you make of your painful experiences, not necessarily dwelling in the muck or murk of suffering.

Once you start a learning process, you can kick off the beginning of an empowered integrity cycle. In this cycle, Integrity Moments build on each other as part of your Personal Tradition of Integrity.

Learning for personal growth and change comes by searching inside, affirming the values and principles that drive your integrity, wrestling with bringing your resistances into awareness, accepting them as part of who you are, and reflecting on the consequences of your actions. Learning comes by reframing and reinterpreting your experience and by widening the lens of how you see to incorporate your peripheral vision. Each allows you to determine new choices for actions to take.

The learning process often involves disclosure, or self-story telling. Remember Lydia's story of dealing with a student's racist remark? Her Big story was consistent with her principles and values. Yet, this moment also presented her with new challenges she hadn't encountered before.

Faced with such a new experience, Lydia told and re-told her story, almost like a personal myth. This story repetition helped build her self-esteem and self-confidence, reinforcing that her intuition and effortful process were appropriate for the situation. That reinforcement of her integrity cycles back, strengthening it.

My hunch is when Lydia faces a similar Integrity Moment, her ability to apply the effort to accomplish another satisfying, consistent experience will be easier. She may also be more likely to self-validate her own experience. With this new experience and her learning, Lydia has started an integrity cycle.

So, too, by gaining confidence in your learning abilities and by reflecting on the power of both your positive and challenging Integrity Moments, you create an integrity cycle of personal learning and growth. Such cycles serve as a key mass of the growing crystal of your Personal Tradition of Integrity.

Needless to say, learning is often an effortful process. You consciously engage in it. The points of the learning process—self-awareness, setting intention, creating choices, courage to commit, action, and learning from consequences—can stand alone. Yet, I hope I have demonstrated how they actually weave together, working as a whole, helping you form habits of integrity.

Specifically, I see the learning process as a spiral, repeating at increasingly deeper levels. With each completed learning process, the integrity cycle is created, then reinforced and grown, forming part of the integrity crystal.

To recap how the crystal grows, first you experience an Integrity Moment. Whether positive or challenging, with reflection, you often learn something about yourself and your choices in that moment. This learning informs the next similar Integrity Moment, creating the beginning of an integrity cycle. The cycle reinforces itself with more positive and related Integrity Moments, forming one facet of the crystal of your Personal Tradition of Integrity.

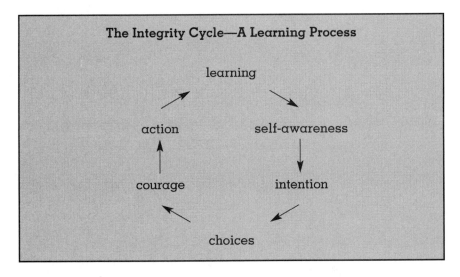

Take a moment now to explore how this learning process fits your experience. Personal Application tools follow. Then in Chapter 9, we will look at how your personal tradition influences the world.

FURTHER READING AND VIEWING

Bateson, M.C. (1994). *Peripheral Visions: Learning Along the Way.* New York: HarperCollins Publishers.

Frankl, V.E. (1959). *Man's Search for Meaning.* New York: Pocket Books.

The King and I (1951). Williamson Music Company.

Orsborn, C. (1992). *Inner Excellence: Spiritual Principles of Life-Driven Business.* San Rafael, CA: New World Library.

Satir, V. (1988). *The New Peoplemaking.* Mountainview, CA: Science and Behavior Books, Inc.

PERSONAL APPLICATION

Recall a Small experience. What were your signals—intuitively, physically, emotionally, mentally, spiritually—that you were Small in this moment?

What will help you pay attention to these signals during the moment so that you can make the Big interpretation?

Now recall a time when you felt oppressed or a victim in a situation. What were your choices during that moment? Challenge yourself to list 8 choices you had during that moment. These choices may be outlandish, funny and reasonable. They may include doing exactly what you did during that circumstance and may also include 'do nothing.'

1.

2.

3.

4.

5.

6.

7.

8.

What choice seems most appealing to you now?

Which choice best promotes an integrity cycle?

PERSONAL APPLICATION

Consider a choice point you are currently facing or an issue that is lively in your life now. Apply the integrity cycle (see the figure on p. 135) to support your decision making. First, briefly describe the situation.

What self-awarenesses do you experience now?

What is your intention? What outcome do you want?

What choices do you have? Brainstorm to generate 8 choices. Select one.

What supports you now in mobilizing your courage? How can you commit?

What action do you want to take?

What consequences do you anticipate?

After you act, note what you learned from the experience.

What can you carry forward to the next similar Integrity Moment?

CHAPTER 9

TAKING YOUR INTEGRITY TO THE WORLD

Buckminster Fuller said, "Integrity is the essence of everything successful." I paraphrase Fuller's statement by suggesting that integrity in action is about being Big in the world.

Integrity is at the core of making your personal and interpersonal worlds work, including enhancing your effectiveness in all the various contexts of your life—family, work, social, relational, community and personal. Integrity is about living a good life.

This chapter wraps up our current exploration of the Integrity Moment by moving into the world with integrity. We explore personal and interpersonal implications, including applications for groups and communities. At the close of the chapter, you have the opportunity to reflect on the implications for your own world of integrity.

PERSONAL SIGNIFICANCE

Claire, the young girl from a small Southern town in the novel *A Place to Call Home*, studies a map that includes her home town and then, dismayed, asks her mother "if we were as small as the map said. 'Don't you worry,' she told me. 'If you study an ant under a magnifying glass, it's as big as an elephant. Size is all in how you look at things, and we're *very* big.'"

Our self-perceptions are key to living with integrity. Perceiving ourselves as Big as an elephant allows us to take action, use our voices, apply effort in meaningful situations, and demonstrate a generosity of spirit to ourselves and others. Further, perceiving ourselves as Big encourages our integrity to grow and develop over time.

Picking up and learning about the growing quartz crystal of our Personal Traditions of Integrity is a significant life adventure. In addition, the learning themes of the Integrity Moment encourage experimenting with the crystal to catch the light in a certain way, shaping the prism of our experience so that we are Big.

Do you know the archetypal assessment tool involving a key and a cup? Close your eyes, and visualize walking along and discovering a key. Join me. See the key in your mind's eye. What does it look like? What do you do with it? Then, continue your stroll, and visualize a cup. What does it look like? What do you do with it?

The archetypal key represents earthly power, and the cup symbolizes knowledge. Do you learn anything about yourself from your visualization? What are your attitudes toward power and knowledge? How do you use them? Each of our keys and cups may look unique, and similarly, your actions are all your own.

As I reflect on the key and the cup, I realize that much of what I have learned about the Integrity Moment involves insight into how we each build and use personal power and self-knowledge. Many stories in this book tell about empowerment and disempowerment, self-knowing and overriding that self-knowing.

Personal power and self-knowledge come from paying attention to the Integrity Moment, the light of the situation that shines on it, and your resulting choices and consequences of those choices that form the prism of your experience. Then, as you apply this learning to your next Integrity Moment, you create an integrity cycle that encourages the growth of your Personal Tradition of Integrity.

As you know, I love hearing stories of Integrity Moments, large and small, everyday and life-changing. What I want is for you to have more Bigness in your day-to-day world. I want you to find and use your keys and cups, to support your choices during Integrity Moments because I believe these are components of being Big and leading a full, rich life.

Often the demands of our lives and on our energy distract us from what's centrally important—acting consistently with our basic principles and values. With refocused attention, we clear up murky pools of confusion with sunlight of clarity and intention.

I hope you find the space to ask yourself important questions during your next Integrity Moment. Do you feel Big now? What is your intention in this moment? What do you really want? What are the choices that can help you be personally powerful in the moment? Does this moment require courage? Do you learn or reinforce something about yourself from this moment?

By starting with ourselves and focusing on having consistency with our core values and principles, we can then enter into all levels of relationships with integrity. The interpersonal implications of integrity are vast, yet I can introduce some of the elements here.

INTERPERSONAL SIGNIFICANCE

We've been focusing on learning from Integrity Moments for personal insight and change. You and I are also instruments for interpersonal change, as well. Several spiritual and psychological traditions suggest that self-awareness and self-care are key for effecting and providing service to others. Our self-awareness and resulting self-care and personal effectiveness create models of success for others.

Whatever your success modelling integrity, you may overestimate your ability to change others. The temptation to change others in your personal relationships, families and workplaces may be high. But the work of successful relationships begins at home, quite literally with yourself.

As discussed in Chapter 8, you have the power to change your own attitude and sense of choicefulness, creating the personal power to effect the strongest family dynamic or most frustrating work relationship. Yet changing others seems so much easier, better. Quite a temptation.

But you cannot change other people. You can only change yourself.

Letting go of the desire to change others may seem paradoxical in light of the desire to influence as one action characteristic of being Big. The difference, I think, centers on the nature of the desire and your intention.

When your desire to influence others comes from your deepest principles and values, you are grounded in your integrity. When you want to change another due to irritation or frustration, you may actually be in a place of blame and judgment.

For example, recently, I found myself transitioning from the blame, judging place to a Big place of influence. I discovered a friend of mine secretly smokes cigarettes. Surprised, my first thought was "that's so disgusting!" and then, "how can you knowingly kill yourself?"

Communicating my first responses to her obviously would be unhelpful and would smack of judgment. Instead, I got in touch with my core values of relationship and clean, healthy living to revise how I wanted to respond. "I really care about you, and I know you know that smoking is dangerous. I really want you to quit. How can I support you?"

Yes, my desire was to influence her. I wanted her to stop smoking. And I could express my desire to influence her without simultaneously blaming or judging her. Both of us can be Big as a result.

Being Big in an Integrity Moment doesn't mean someone else has to be Small. Bigness does not come in a fixed amount. It's not a scarce resource. In fact, the abundance theory applies. I can be even Bigger in my world when I create opportunities for others to be Big.

On an interpersonal level, whether in an intimate relationship, with a friend or family member, or in your organizational life, you bring yourself and your Integrity Moments with you. Rather than concentrating so hard on changing others, focus on who you are and what's important to you. What changes can you make in yourself that may happily and inadvertently change others?

Recently, my parents came to visit me in my newly renovated home. During my adult years, my relationship with my father has had tensions, born of love and expressed by both of us out of intention to change the other. With support from my coach, I clearly set my intention to have a different kind of time together—one that was at least pleasant and filled with patience.

That visit proved to be one of the pivotal experiences of my life. Inviting my parents to stay in my space, itself created with such loving, soulful intention, was powerful in and of itself. As our time together progressed, my father made random comments to me. "I'm so comfortable here. This is like being at home."

After watching me facilitate our book club meeting, he remarked, "I can see you're really good at what you do." Later in the visit, seated in my office, he said, "you are as different from your brothers as night and day."

While seemingly small, these remarks demonstrated that my father really saw me for who I am. He acknowledged my Authentic Self for perhaps the first time in my life. I felt so loved. And I like to think he felt loved by me.

What happened? Neither of us tried to change the other. We simply enjoyed being with each other. This state of being, rather than actively trying to manipulate the other, allowed us both to be genuine and loving. A truly remarkable Big moment for each of us.

My hope is this book greases the hinges for easily opening the door to living with more integrity in the moment. The more you fully bring yourself to your Integrity Moments, the more you can use your generosity of spirit to support others to be Big as well, as my father and I did for each other.

STRATEGY TIME

Take stock of who in your life you want to change. If only so-and-so would change, life would be great. Notice how many people just like so-and-so have shown up in your life. Perhaps you attract these types of people.

Learn why you may be attracting these people to you. They keep showing up to teach you something about yourself. Success with them is not about changing them. It's about changing you.

What value or principle gets hooked by so-and-so? In what ways does your relationship with so-and-so leave you feeling Small? Are you reacting out of habit? Does being with so-and-so lead you to criticize yourself in some ways? These insights provide a great starting point for your learning.

Use that learning to set new intentions. For example, how do you want particular relationships to move forward? Evaluate what choices you have to re-establish your Big-ness. Have the courage to commit to one of the choices, experiment, and learn what happens. Be open to healing, restoring and reinvigorating your relationship.

INTEGRITY AND INTERPERSONAL CONSISTENCY

As explored in Chapter 1, integrity is often defined in terms of keeping commitments, acting consistently over time, and following through on what you say. Interpersonal relationships, in whatever settings, rely on such relational credibility.

Perhaps, on some level, you have become numb to the inconsistencies in your world. Hyper-media attention reveals the challenges our political leaders face day-to-day to behave consistently with their family values. Campaign pledges often fall by the wayside in light of political realities.

But most likely, you still expect your organizational leaders to act consistently with their words and the workplace values, despite the challenges they may be facing as they interpret their situations. We still want consistency in our personal worlds.

So how you stand up for your beliefs and handle your inconsistencies from one Integrity Moment to the next are also part of establishing trust and credibility in your relationships. In your workplace, your social life, and your family, your individual and collective well-being rely on relationships in which you can truly be yourself, act out of integrity, risk making mistakes, and take a stand to optimize your life—all courageous acts.

Recognizing and learning from your Integrity Moments, both individually and collaboratively, help create such relationships. The factors which promote or inhibit your acting with integrity in the moment also effect your relationships day-to-day. How can you address what you learn in these moments with everyone involved to create personal and collective integrity? How can you all emerge Big?

The simple answer is by beginning with yourself. What you and I learn on an individual level about our Integrity Moments applies to interpersonal relationships as well, including groups such as workplace teams, family systems and social organizations.

FOR GROUPS OF ALL KINDS

One place that I've been most challenged to hold myself Big in the Integrity Moment has been group settings. Interpreting the group's culture and norms that guide behavior in the group has often had the effect of leaving me Small.

What I now know is that beginning with myself, focusing on what is important to me and who I am during this moment, provides a framework for my participation that opens rather than diminishes opportunities. By being Big in the moment, I may serve as a pivotal person for another, spark an intuitive insight, and facilitate conversation in a Big-making way.

Recently, I joined a professional association committee with the intention to influence the work and its outcome. I was acting on very strong beliefs and principles and knew that my decision to be a part of the committee came from a place of integrity.

What I notice is that my intentions are clear to other committee members because I have chosen to communicate them directly. I've taken a stand for standards I believe in. This committee work is directly related to how I see myself as a Life Coach, therefore my work identity, and I have disclosed this meaning to the others involved.

Engaging in the work has been satisfying because my sharing allowed others to express their points of view, too. Our differences are stated and respected. We proceed with the work, with more complete knowledge of our differing backgrounds, motivations, and expectations—all aspects of former traps for me.

By intentionally being Big, I believe I have contributed to a Big team environment that cycles and reinforces Bigness. Plus, I'm starting to build my muscle for being Big in groups.

Think back on your own Integrity Moments. How many of them involve your family, membership in a group or team, or center on your world of work or organizations? What have you learned to apply to these settings?

IN OUR COMMUNITIES

In Chapter 6, we discussed how integrity is the action negotiation between the authentic part of 'me' and the social-ethical part of 'me-in-community.' What does it mean to be fully who we are and be Big in our community?

A recent study of young gang members shows they have very high opinions of themselves and therefore feel entitled to break laws. Martin Seligman relays how self-esteem is not about inflated self-opinion, but rather is centered on feeling good about what you do. I restate that as perceiving yourself to be Big with integrity.

Being Big in your community then is about feeling good about what you do. For me, that includes not littering, recycling, smiling and greeting passersby, and giving a neighbor a ride to the airport. For others, volunteering for a neighborhood association, participating in a street block party, and coaching a girls soccer team are all about being Big in community.

Communities such as men's and women's support groups, spiritual groups, and study circles also present identity-building and Big-making opportunities. Gardening clubs, PTAs, bowling leagues, and other activity-based groups bring people together to explore commonalities and differences in ways that support and sustain our integrity.

STRATEGY TIME

Are there any groups or communities you belong to in which you feel Small? If so, follow the integrity cycle. Commend yourself for being aware that you have the opportunity to convert your experience to being Big.

Get clear about your intention. What outcomes and goals did you have when you joined the group? Have these shifted? Based on your intention now, what choices do you have? Make sure to name at least three, so that you fully elevate all the options available to you.

Which option best satisfies your intention? What's involved in committing to action? If there are obstacles, how many of these are people you are trying to change? Relax and let that one go, just as an experiment. You can take up the old strategy again anytime you choose.

Are the obstacles internal? Is there a pattern of fear, mistrust or another Small theme you recognize as being all yours? If so, congratulate yourself again on that awareness. Awareness is the first step toward self-change. Explore your Big options. Experiment. What you have to gain is so much more compelling than what you have to lose.

TAKE WINGS AND FLY

One academic community, a group of neuroscientists who study the brain and central nervous system, present an interesting paradox. Their recent, provocative studies suggest that morality is genetic and that the soul is imprinted with genetic history and evolution.

If these neuroscientists are correct, then physical mechanisms actually determine our behavior. And this book is moot. So the paradoxes of life go. Your challenge, regardless, is to live the best life you can, consistent as often as possible with your basic values and principles.

Beyond my expectations, studying the Integrity Moment has changed how I experience myself in my world. I clearly see the possibilities for you, for me and for us. I believe in your personal greatness as expressed in your Integrity Moments. I feel so full:

The fence surrounds me.
I push hard to open the gate
and release the floods.

Like Alice returning from Wonderland, we bring what we have learned on our journeys back with us. Thank you for adventuring with me. Be Big!

FURTHER READING

Baumeister, R.F., Boden, J.M., & Smart, L. (1996). Relation of Threatened Egotism to Violence and Aggression: The Dark Side of High Self-Esteem. *Psychological Review, 103, 1*, 5–33.

Posner, B.Z., Kouzes, J.M., & Schmidt, W.H. (1985). Shared Values Make a Difference: An Empirical Test of Corporate Culture. *Human Resource Management, 24, 3*, 293–309.

Seligman, M.E.P. (1996). *The Optimistic Child.* New York: Harper Perennial.

Smith, D. (1997). *A Place to Call Home.* New York: Bantam Books.

Wolfe, T. (1997). Sorry, Your Soul Just Died. *The Oregonian*, Forum, 5/11/97.

PERSONAL APPLICATION

Think of a family situation you are currently facing. How can you be fully who you are and be Big in this situation? What are your choices?

Now recall another interpersonal situation that challenges you. What are your choices here? What implications and consequences do these choices entail?

Perhaps you have a work situation or community issue to reflect on. What have you learned from this book that will support you in this situation?

For more information about Linda Tobey's workshops, please call (202) 232-1824, email *linda@life-foundations.com*, or visit *www.life-foundations.com*

If you would like to order additional copies of *The Integrity Moment*, please call 1-800-338-8290 or use this order form and mail to Kendall/Hunt Publishing Company, Customer Service, 4050 Westmark Drive, Dubuque, IA 52004.

Qty	Title/ISBN	Price*	Total
	The Integrity Moment ISBN: 0-7872-8128-X	$15.95	

*Price subject to change without notice.

AL, AZ, CA, CO, FL, GA, IA, IL, IN, KS, KY, LA, MA, MD, MI, MN, MO, NC, NJ, NM, NY, OH, PA, TN, TX, VA, WA, & WI please add appropriate sales tax.

U.S. Postage: Add $4 shipping for the first unit, and $0.50 each for additional units. Postage outside the U.S. will be charged accordingly.

☐ Check or money order enclosed (payable to Kendall/Hunt)
☐ Charge my credit card: ☐ VISA   ☐ MasterCard   ☐ AmEx

Account # _____ Exp. Date _____

Signature _____

Name _____

Address _____

City _____ State _____ Zip_____

Phone_____ Email _____